Teaching Mindfulness to Teens as a Path of Empowerment

Teaching Mindfulness to Teens as a Path of Empowerment

Meghan LeBorious

ROWMAN & LITTLEFIELD
Lanham • Boulder • New York • London

Published by Rowman & Littlefield
An imprint of The Rowman & Littlefield Publishing Group, Inc.
4501 Forbes Boulevard, Suite 200, Lanham, Maryland 20706
www.rowman.com

86-90 Paul Street, London EC2A 4NE

Copyright © 2024 by Meghan LeBorious

All rights reserved. No part of this book may be reproduced in any form or by any electronic or mechanical means, including information storage and retrieval systems, without written permission from the publisher, except by a reviewer who may quote passages in a review.

British Library Cataloguing in Publication Information Available

Library of Congress Cataloging-in-Publication Data

Names: LeBorious, Meghan, author.
Title: Teaching mindfulness to teens as a path of empowerment / Meghan LeBorious.
Description: Lanham, Maryland : Rowman & Littlefield, [2024] | Includes bibliographical references. | Summary: "Teaching Mindfulness to Teens as a Path of Empowerment is a teacher-level perspective on mindfulness instruction with systems-level implications. It lays the groundwork for a thriving, highly engaging, student-centered, antiracist mindfulness classroom that serves every student in realizing their full potential"— Provided by publisher.
Identifiers: LCCN 2023054595 (print) | LCCN 2023054596 (ebook) | ISBN 9781475874143 (cloth) | ISBN 9781475874150 (paperback) | ISBN 9781475874167 (epub)
Subjects: LCSH: Teenagers—Education—United States. | Mindfulness (Psychology) | Emotional intelligence. | Power (Social sciences) | Self-care, Health. | Teacher-student relationships. | Community and school. | Culturally relevant pedagogy.
Classification: LCC LB1737.U6 L43 2024 (print) | LCC LB1737.U6 (ebook) | DDC 373.1801/9—dc23/eng/20240116
LC record available at https://lccn.loc.gov/2023054595
LC ebook record available at https://lccn.loc.gov/2023054596

For my son, Simon, who inspires me every day
and gives me hope for the future.

Contents

Foreword		ix
Acknowledgments		xi
Introduction		xiii
1	Mindfulness Definitions and Brain Science	1
2	Building Community and Restorative Justice	7
3	Why Nuanced Representation Matters in Mindfulness Classrooms and Beyond	15
4	Instruction	21
5	Making It Engaging	31
6	Elevating Student Voice and Leadership	39
7	Working with Resistance	43
8	Mindfulness Instruction	53
9	Trauma-Sensitive Practice and Why Embodiment Matters	65
10	Dealing with Difficult Emotions and Discomfort	73
11	Right Emphasis and the Importance of Emphasizing Authenticity Over Positivity	79
12	Culturally Responsive and Antiracist Practice	83
13	Creating Meaning with Ritual	87
14	Engaging Families as Partners	91

Conclusion 97

Appendices
  A: Meditation Techniques and Basic Instructions 99
  B: Mindful Minute Student Script 103
  C: Mindfulness Elective—Sample Scope and Sequence 105
  D: Sample Mindfulness Course Standards 109
  E: Steps for What Students Can Do If Triggered During Practice 111

Bibliography 113

Foreword

Life has a way of weaving people and experiences together in the most unexpected and transformative manner. As I stand at the threshold of introducing this book on mindfulness, authored by the remarkable Meghan LeBorious, who I call Ms. L., my heart swells with gratitude and reverence for the profound influence she has had on my journey. It is an honor to share a glimpse of the immense impact her teachings have had on me as I invite you to embark on a path that has the potential to reshape your understanding of life itself.

Ms. L.—a beacon of wisdom, a guiding light, and an embodiment of mindfulness—entered my life at a juncture when I was grappling with the cacophony of modern existence. The moments of tranquility were fleeting, buried under the avalanche of responsibilities, worries, and distractions. It was in the midst of this chaos that Ms. L.'s mindfulness class emerged like an oasis—an opportunity to explore the depths of presence and reclaim the beauty of each passing moment.

Under Ms. L.'s compassionate guidance, I delved into the profound meaning of mindfulness, a concept far richer and more nuanced than I had ever imagined. Through her teachings, I learned that mindfulness was not just about meditation or moments of stillness; it was a tapestry woven with threads of awareness, intention, and compassion. Ms. L. effortlessly bridged the gap between the theoretical and the practical, gently steering us toward a way of life that embraced mindfulness in its entirety.

My definition of mindfulness has changed many times over the years and it is still evolving. Mindfulness is peace—peace with yourself and those around you. Mindfulness is true serenity. It is being able to come to terms with your emotions and experience them with an open mind. It is understanding that all emotions are valid and deserve a space to live in your mind—a space to be explored and appreciated. It is taking the time to heal, grow, and become stronger with the knowledge of how to address your feelings.

As the weeks turned into months under Ms. L.'s tutelage, I began to notice profound transformations taking root within me. The tendrils of stress that once ensnared my thoughts began to loosen their grip. The beauty of life's simplest moments—an unhurried sip of tea, the play of sunlight on leaves—captivated my attention. The chaos of life remained, but my response to it shifted; I found myself embracing challenges with a newfound sense of equanimity.

When I was a senior, I became a student assistant teacher in one of Ms. L's mindfulness classes. I helped with teaching the younger students, and with planning and designing the class. It was nice to watch all the things that I learned being taught to the younger kids and to see how they internalized it. Just watching their words change in how they described things showed their growth and understanding of mindfulness and its practices.

I just finished my first year of college. All I could do was think about all these practices as the workload became overwhelming. I just let myself understand that it wasn't something I could change so I decided to apply what I knew. I took time to understand that and breathe, along with other stuff, and got right back to all the things that seemed impossible. These abilities won't ever leave me, as they have now become habits.

This book, penned by the very hand that guided me through this transformation, is a testament to Ms. L.'s dedication and wisdom. As you peruse its pages, you hold a treasure trove of insights and practices that have the potential to unveil the beauty of mindfulness in your own life and how it is important to teach these methods to children and teens. May Ms. L.'s words resonate as deeply with you as they have with me, and may this book be a guiding companion on your journey toward embracing each moment with a heart full of presence and guiding students to do the same.

With profound gratitude and the spirit of mindfulness,
Gayana Maelle

Acknowledgments

I acknowledge the traditional custodians of the lands that held me as I wrote this book—the Lenape people of the New York City region; and the Podunk and Paugussett people of the Connecticut region.

I also acknowledge my privilege as a white person in a society that preferences the needs of white people; and I acknowledge that it has been easier for me to develop and deliver my vision, including writing this book, because of this privilege.

For support with developing these ideas and bringing them to the world, I'm immensely grateful to friends, mentors, and colleagues Dr. Nayira Polanco, PhD, Kari O'Driscoll, Julie Stuart, Ursula Koffer, Tracy Heilers, Tovi Scruggs-Hussein, Khayree Bey, Ray Diaz, Rocco Gentile, Elizabeth Rodriguez, Sasha O'Connor, Fanny Hodges, Todd Serman, Dominique Cocklin, David Rohlfing, Melissa Campbell, Dale Marshall, Jessica Ciardullo, Alan Brown, Kaira Jewel Lingo, Katrina Harriman, Paula Grant, Jennifer Reno, Eileen Fisher, Kristin Santa Maria, Stephanie Diamond, Kierra Foster-Ba, Kateri Kennedy, Melissa Jean-Baptiste, Tammy Burstein, Peter Fodera, Melissa Michaels, PhD, Gina Sharpe, Sharon Salzberg, Gabrielle Roth, Chögyam Trungpa Rinpoche, Eric Spiegel, Shana Harris, Mary Bergstrom, Jonathan Chajet, Elisa Matula, Gianna Gonzalez, Moira Tierney, Mary Sue Connolly, Dharma Fredericks, Brigid Rowan, Cavel Khan, Christina Hunter-Khan, Lana Yusupova, Katerina Vemic, Dr. Veronica Marion, PhD, Dr. Judy Carson, PhD, Barnaby Spring, and to my former principal, Anna-Maria Mulé, who supported me in building a thriving mindfulness program even though there was a towering list of competing priorities.

Thank you to former students Zariah Casillas, Gianni Douglas, Gayana Maelle, Diamond Caban, Jennivie Wilson, Kaydian Wilson, Obdulia Zuluaga, Amani Lewis, Cree Washington, Hannah Medor, Ibrahim Fudol, Celena Kisoon, Jamya White, Naomi Williams, Mea Richards, Elia Riebl, Aden Bachan, and countless others who have inspired me and helped to shape this vision.

Thanks to Tom Koerner and Jasmine Holman of Rowman & Littlefield for your belief in and support of this book.

And I can't possibly express the depth of my thanks to my family. To my parents, who have worked tirelessly and often thanklessly for decades in hope for a better world, to my mother, Betsy LeBorious, for her mentorship around engaging families as partners, and her creative, passionate approach to everything, and to my father, Richard LeBorious, for his boundless integrity and tender heart, to my sister, Courtney LeBorious-Eder, and her husband, Stephen Eder, for hosting me during this writing and for their tireless, skillful support, to my playful and generous brother, Devon LeBorious, my wonderful nieces Maya Grigely and Joie Eder, my nephew Eric McArthur, and all my nieces and nephews. And boundless gratitude to my aunts, uncles, cousins, and ancestors. And special thanks to my not-husband, Eulas Pizarro, who listened patiently, pushed back skillfully, and supported me tirelessly.

And thanks most of all to my son, Simon Pizarro, for his excellent sense of humor, for his ability to see what's real, for being there with me throughout this process, and for teaching me every day.

Introduction

Mindfulness helps you be more in reality.

—Nia Gomez, high school student

Mindfulness is beneficial to my health because it helps my heart not get rotten.

—Obdulia Zuluaga, high school student

Teaching mindfulness to teens of color in NYC has been a labor of love.

This book is a series of personal essays drawing on my own experiences of teaching mindfulness to teens. I am not an academic, a trauma expert, a researcher, or a psychotherapist. I'm just a dedicated high school teacher who was able to build up a mindfulness program in my school over the course of several years in response to a need that I saw.

Each essay is designed to stand alone, so there may be some redundancies. Many of the topics are braided tightly together, including working with resistance, engaging students, elevating student voice, building community, and why nuanced representation matters in our classrooms. Every one of these topics is intended to support antiracist classrooms and practices and should be constantly evaluated with this lens.

I acknowledge my privilege in stepping into this role. As a white person in a white supremacist society, it was easier for me to be assertive in creating a mindfulness program than it would have been for some of my highly qualified colleagues of color. In addition, as a result of ongoing systemic racism, it was easier for me to become a teacher than for many. I also acknowledge that being a white person teaching primarily students of color in a white dominant school system is inherently problematic.

In the words of Ibram X. Kendi, "The opposite of racist isn't 'not racist.' It's 'antiracist.'"[1] Not being racist isn't enough. We need to actively examine everything we do for its intentions and impacts.

In one school, we had a field trip policy that required every student to get every teacher to sign a permission slip before they would be allowed to attend. The stated intention was to motivate kids to complete their classwork, but it was demoralizing for (often Black or brown) kids to go to their (often white) teacher and in some cases get rejected. After a while, those who already saw themselves as "bad" didn't even bother, since they didn't want to give the teacher the power of saying no. The kids who most needed to feel included were marginalized and shut down, damaging them and the overall community. Seeing the impacts of this policy over several years made it clear it was having a racist impact, and that it needed to be changed.

Mindfulness instruction can support the cause of antiracism if it emphasizes empowerment, agency, and self-healing, and supports students in stepping into their power. If it is used as a means of crowd control or to insist on a certain teacher's values, it can, however, support racism, so we need to be constantly examining and adapting our practices.

Initially, becoming a teacher was a painful shock to my system. It definitely did not feel like I was supposed to be empowering students. I changed careers from being a freelance designer and visual artist in my late thirties, and found myself suddenly in a much harsher reality. I struggled to find my footing, but felt more and more like I was drowning in quicksand as I, myself, became an agent of "the system" despite my best intentions to bring benefit to my students.

By the time I became a public school teacher, I already had strong practices in a Buddhist meditation tradition, as well as in a dance and movement meditation tradition. Although I did not talk about any of this at work, these practices helped me process my feelings, experience community, and connect with a deeper sense of meaning, even when day-to-day life in my school felt agonizing.

Though no doubt some of what I was experiencing in practice carried over into the classroom, I never thought it would be possible to bring meditation to my students. At that point, mindfulness and meditation were still seen by some as threatening to certain religions. And mindfulness was often seen as flaky, new-agey, ultra-white bullshit. And no one would ever say this, but there were some who weren't interested in empowering kids or treating their suffering as a real experience; in fact sometimes the opposite seemed true.

Still, I signed up for an intensive six-week online course with Mindful Schools in California to learn to teach secular meditation to youth just in case someday space miraculously opened up.

I began to teach tiny bits of mindfulness tucked into the edges of my classes. Gradually over the next decade, I was able to build a mindfulness program by looking for empty spaces I could flow into, and adding one piece at a time, with the support and collaboration of my administrators.

In its fullest expression, I taught every ninth grade student in my high school every day for the entire year. At this point, if I had won the lottery, I would have still done my job. Although in a perfect world, students wouldn't need a class like this, it was an incredible honor and a privilege to hold space in this way; and I was brought to tears regularly as I witnessed students in healing themselves and one another, and finding capacities they had shut down or never connected with.

My own journey as an adolescent was painful. By my early teens, I had started to drink heavily, and to accumulate trauma that resulted from my reckless behavior. The anxiety and shame arising from my experiences at this time led me to drink even more to dull the seemingly unbearable feelings. There was also something unexamined in me that wanted to replay the same story but get a different ending, which, of course, got the opposite result.

When that didn't work, I became performative, trying to convince myself and others that I was a free spirit. Instead of being free, I was a prisoner of persistent anxiety. It controlled all of my words and actions. I would do anything to try to escape the pain I carried around. Once I called a friend nonstop for several hours straight, letting the phone ring and the voicemail pick up, then hanging up and immediately calling again. I simply could not sit with my own discomfort.

I became myopic and self-centered, always evaluating things in relation to my own ego needs. Trauma and its accompanists got more and more complex, and more and more written into my identity and body. I'm not proud to share that I caused a lot of harm to myself and others.

If someone had taught me about trauma and its impacts; if I had ever considered the idea that it was possible to pause and hold my discomfort, to not *do*; if I had learned that emotions have a purpose and that they can be tolerated—that would have changed things for me.

I have tried to create the class, to create the *process* really, that I needed as a teen.

The teens I work with today face all of the same challenges I faced plus additional pressures, including screens and social media, environmental chaos, a volatile political climate, along with psychological impacts from the COVID-19 pandemic.

Even before the pandemic, the CDC reported that for adolescents, constant feelings of sadness or hopelessness increased by almost 40 percent between 2009–2019.[2] Since that time, mental health issues, especially depression and anxiety, have continued to spike. Between 2017 and 2019, nearly one in ten youth ages twelve to seventeen attempted suicide.[3]

On top of all of that, most of the teens I work with are people of color, as is my own son. In addition to the stress of being a teen at this moment in history, many have the added burden of coping with the impacts of structural and personal racism.

When I remember how much pain I was in as a teen, then add on all of these additional layers, it feels hard to breathe.

We owe it to our youth to do everything we can to help them heal themselves and give them the tools they need to find their way.

In the very beginning, when I would push into other people's classrooms during my lunch once a week to teach mindfulness, I had data to show it was having at least some impact. These small interventions can be very important. The difference between zero mindfulness instruction and a little bit of instruction is massive.

But when I switched from once a week to teaching full-time mindfulness classes, things got real. There was just no comparison. Helping students to move through a patient, intentional process and find their way to the other side made a noticeable difference for many.

I continue to be amazed and still don't fully understand how this magic works, but student feedback is clear, as you'll read in students' own words throughout the book.

Our youth urgently need spaces and intentional processes to support them in healing themselves from trauma, individuating, finding their unique expression, and stepping into their power.

I know this is asking a lot of us. I know schools have limited resources, limited staff, and infinite mandates. But creating meaningful spaces and processes, not just in fits and starts, not just added on top of the already towering stack of teacher requirements, is essential if our kids are to thrive.

So why am I doing this? Because I want to have impact and joy, and because even in the face of withering oppression, and the agony of my role in it, I have hope.

Why do I believe in meaningful mindfulness instruction for every child? Because I believe in the fundamentally intact power and grace of each of our beautiful children; and I'm tired of witnessing the ongoing brutality, the silenced voices, the loss of hope, the pinched shoulders, the hoods up, and the knit brows of children who would be our geniuses, our healers, and our guides.

The future demands it of us. May we hear its call. And may all of our children and all beings thrive, today and always.

NOTES

1. Ibram X. Kendi, *How to Be an Antiracist* (New York: One World, 2019).

2. Sherry Everett Jones et al., "Mental Health, Suicidality, and Connectedness Among High School Students During the COVID-19 Pandemic—Adolescent Behaviors and Experiences Survey, United States, January–June 2021," Centers for Disease Control and Prevention, April 1, 2022, https://www.cdc.gov/mmwr/volumes/71/su/su7103a3.htm#:~:text=and%20Mental%20Health-,Compared%20with%20those%20who%20did%20not%20feel%20close%20to%20persons,35.4%25%20versus%2052.9%25)%2C%20of

3. Asha V. Ivey-Stephenson et al., "Suicidal Ideation and Behaviors among High School Students—Youth Risk Behavior Survey, United States, 2019," Centers for Disease Control and Prevention, August 20, 2020, https://www.cdc.gov/mmwr/volumes/69/su/su6901a6.htm

Chapter One

Mindfulness Definitions and Brain Science

> Mindfulness is being attentive. Mindfulness involves paying attention to your environment, for example, the sounds you're hearing and the way the chair you're sitting in feels. Mindfulness is also centered on acknowledging the way you're feeling on the inside, whether it be difficult emotions or the way your surroundings make you feel.
>
> —Kaydian Wilson, high school student

Mindfulness is a quality of mind. Meditation and mindfulness are sometimes used as synonyms, but they are not the same thing. Meditations are actions and processes we undertake to intentionally cultivate certain states of mind.

Mindfulness is a particular *quality* of mind—the result of brain training—that allows us to be with our present-moment unfolding experiences, including thoughts, sensations, and events in our environment, even as all of it arises and changes. It is being in reality and in the dance of life without reservation, and without the constraint of the stories we constantly produce that keep us small, separate, stuck, and afraid.

Mindfulness is an innate human quality, but it is obscured to varying degrees in most of us. The practice of cultivating mindfulness is really more about removing the things that block it than about bringing in something different.

To convey the felt sense of what mindfulness is to teens, we could say, "You know how it is when you're reading a book and you get to the bottom of the page, and you have *absolutely* no idea what you just read?" When there are nods and raised hands we could add, "That thing that got lost, that was mindfulness. And the thing that *noticed* that it got lost, well, that was mindfulness, too."

Students may start out with one definition of mindfulness, but their personal definition is sure to shift and evolve many times in the course of a mindfulness class and within their own practice. "Mindfulness is peace with yourself," one student shared at the end of a semester. "And mindfulness is peace with others," another added.

Although mindfulness is a specific quality of mind and that's how it will be used here, in the context of school policies the definition might be expanded to include related social and emotional topics, as well as the spaces and practices that promote well-being.

A very few people never practice meditation yet are able to spend their lives in a state of blissful mindfulness; but most of us need intentional practices to cultivate our ability to be mindful.

This is where meditation comes in. There are many forms of meditation, but the ones I'm most familiar with all start with learning to direct the mind toward a certain object.

Some common objects we could choose to focus on include our breathing or the sounds in our environment. To cultivate mindfulness, we point our attention toward this chosen object again and again, noticing when we become distracted and gently shepherding attention back to this focus. Bringing our attention to the chosen object helps to stabilize the mind. But it is both noticing that we are noticing the object, *and* noticing the shifts in our attention when we are *not* noticing the object—along with an attitude of curiosity and nonjudgment—that is the essence of mindfulness practice.

In bringing our attention back to the object we chose, we short-circuit the mind's tendency to take us out of reality with its overthinking, stories, planning, and regretting. By repeating this process again and again, we develop the ability to be in the present moment, even when it is uncomfortable, boring, or painful. Although this does mean we will more acutely notice our difficult feelings, it also gives us greater access to joy, motivation, and intimacy.

Meditation without mindfulness is like reading endless cookbooks without ever cooking anything. Developing the quality of mindfulness is what really matters for our purposes, and is the thing that has the power to deeply transform our experience.[1] It opens the doorway to everything else we might study in mindfulness class, including accessing flow states, regulating emotions, having a growth mindset, making responsible decisions, building up our relationships, being able to communicate and listen deeply, and experiencing real joy from time to time.

In the process of practicing mindfulness, we begin to notice the irrational stories our mind comes up with when we are not focused on the primary object we chose. Sometimes these stories may not have previously been at the level of conscious thought. Noticing our thoughts begins to give us some space from them, and lessens the stranglehold these stories have on our experience, our decisions, and on our sense of who we think we are.

With practice, the mind begins to settle down, and its contents become more and more visible.

This all happens quite naturally. All we have to do is commit to the noticing. The rest unfolds on its own.

• • •

Mindfulness is a component of virtually every religious practice and spiritual methodology, including Christian, Muslim, Buddhist, Hindu, Jewish, and Indigenous religions, but it is not particular to any of these systems.

The system that has spent the most time specifically creating methods for developing mindfulness over the course of thousands of years is Buddhism. Secular mindfulness traditions in the West owe a debt of gratitude to Buddhism, especially as it has been articulated in Southeast Asian practices.

Secular practice traditions have looked beneath religious aspects of Buddhism to mindfulness itself and sought to make mindfulness available to all people, regardless of religious affiliation.

In the 1960s and 1970s Buddhist meditation practices began to find their way to America. Jon Kabat-Zinn, an American meditation practitioner, spent several years in retreat in Southeast Asia. A doctor, when he returned to America, he initiated mindfulness practices to help patients who were experiencing severe pain and documented notable improvements.

Although there were undoubtedly people of diverse backgrounds already practicing some form of meditation in America at that time, it was the work of Jon Kabat-Zinn that was built on by educational leaders to bring secular mindfulness to students in school settings starting around 2007.

At first, it met with occasional resistance, as some pushed back, fearing that secular mindfulness and meditation were an affront to certain religions.

But as time has progressed, there is more and more evidence about the positive impacts of secular mindfulness and meditation for both youth and adult practitioners, and more and more school leaders have bought in. Studies published between 2009–2023 in *Psychological Bulletin*, *School Psychology Quarterly*, and other journals indicate that students who receive mindfulness instruction tend to have better focus,[2] more ability to self-regulate,[3] less stress, and fewer incidents that lead to disciplinary consequences.[4] In addition, some studies indicate that mindfulness interventions improve symptoms of anxiety and depression in young people.[5]

Research is ongoing, and continued studies are needed to understand the nuances around how and when to employ mindfulness to support teen mental health, along with its limitations. Even so, there appear to be enough positive indicators that mindfulness, although not a panacea, stands to benefit our youth and help them cope better with both daily pressures and painful experiences.

• • •

There are many resources that map the biological impacts of mindfulness practice, including the ways that it impacts the brain.

This is very simplified, but here are some aspects of brain science that can be highlighted for teens.

The body has two systems that talk back and forth with each other: the sympathetic nervous system (the fight-flight-freeze system) and the parasympathetic nervous system (the calm-down system).

The sympathetic nervous system is also called the fight-flight-freeze system. The center of the sympathetic nervous system is a tiny brain structure called the amygdala that's located deep inside the middle of the brain. This part of the brain is also called the "lizard brain" because the first humans, even as far back as cave people, had this part of the brain. Back then, they didn't do much higher-level thinking, and this lizard brain was all about keeping them alive. It's the survival part. It's in charge of the fight-flight-freeze response. It gets us ready if we need to fight; to flee—that's when you run away, that's the flight part; or to freeze—like a rabbit, thinking it won't be seen if it doesn't move.

These are all ancient human survival instincts that are part of our brain. This is the part of the brain that keeps us on high alert, like if we have to jump out of the way of a racing bus that's about to hit us. It also pumps out all kinds of powerful body chemicals that get us ready to fight, flee, or freeze.

For many of us, the amygdala kicks in even when we're not in danger, trying all the time to keep us safe. It also keeps us tensed up in a state of high anxiety, watching for the next threat.

Sometimes we need the fight-flight-freeze response, but many of us have forgotten how to turn it off *ever*, making it difficult to relax. It also makes it hard for us to learn, form close relationships, and experience joy. So if our brain is always keeping us in fight-flight-freeze mode, we miss out on a lot of things.

Regular mindfulness practice leads to a decrease in the size of the amygdala, the lizard part of the brain that is involved in the fight-flight-freeze response.[6] This means that our brain isn't constantly turning on the freak-out response, even when we don't need it. It means that the fight-flight-freeze system isn't running our program every single minute. That's all the fight-flight-freeze system, or sympathetic nervous system, controls—and it's not just our brain but all over the body, in our muscles, bones, heart, and nerves.

The parasympathetic nervous system, otherwise known as the calm-down system, does the opposite. It helps the body regulate, calms down the racing heart, and relaxes the muscles. It allows us to settle the body, giving us access to different parts of the brain, not just the lizard part.

Practicing mindfulness strengthens the calm-down system.

Practicing mindfulness is also associated with an increase in brain material and brain cell connections in the front of the brain, the region called the prefrontal lobes. This area is associated with judgment, empathy, and creative thinking.[7]

Ideally our survival brain—our flight-flight-freeze brain—kicks in fast when we need it, like when a bus is about to hit us; then it turns off and the parasympathetic nervous system takes over and calms us down quickly, giving us access to our full inner resources.

Another thing you need to know is about how brain structures change according to what you do. Anything we do with our brain gets stronger because brain pathways are built up with new cells and connections that get added when we do that thing.

So if we want to get good at worrying, the best thing to do is worry a lot.

If we want to get good at listening compassionately to our friends, the best way to do that is to practice listening compassionately often.

Whatever we practice will get stronger.

Brain scientists like to say, "What fires together, wires together."[8] That is to say, whatever the brain does, we are creating pathways in the brain for the brain to keep doing that thing.

That doesn't mean we should try to shut down painful emotions or negative thoughts, though. That isn't actually helpful.

But it does mean that if we practice mindfulness regularly, we can start to train the brain so it doesn't overthink as much. Every time we're practicing and we let go of overthinking and return back to the breath or whatever our primary object is, we're cutting the root of overthinking away.

That's why the more times we practice bringing the brain back to the breath or whatever primary object we picked for our meditation, the better the mind gets at being in the present moment.

Students have often shared that this material is important for making them feel like there is a purpose for learning about and practicing mindfulness.

Teaching this basic brain science right in the beginning of the class with rich images and opportunities for students to find their own way into the concepts sets the stage for engagement. It's also helpful to teach the concept of neuroplasticity, recognizing that the brain is constantly changing based on what we do with it, perhaps in the context of growth mindset.[9] These ideas can be reinforced again and again in class discussions, and in synthesis and reflection questions throughout the course.

NOTES

1. Bhante Gunaratana, *Mindfulness in Plain English* (Somerville: Wisdom, 2019).
2. Alberto Chiesa and Alessandro Serretti, "Mindfulness-Based Stress Reduction for Stress Management in Healthy People: A Review and Meta-Analysis," *Journal of Alternative and Complementary Medicine* 15, no. 5 (May 2009): 593–600, https://doi.org/10.1089/acm.2008.0495
3. Lizabeth Roemer, Sarah Krill Williston, and Laura Grace Rollins, "Mindfulness and Emotion Regulation," *Current Opinion in Psychology* 3 (June 2015): 52–57, https://doi.org/10.1016/j.copsyc.2015.02.006
4. Xiang Zhou et al., "Effects of Mindfulness-Based Stress Reduction on Anxiety Symptoms in Young People: A Systematic Review and Meta-Analysis," *Psychiatry Research* 289, no. 113002 (July 2020), https://doi.org/10.1016/j.psychres.2020.113002
5. Anne Trafton, "Two Studies Reveal Benefits of Mindfulness for Middle School Students," MIT News, August 26, 2019, https://news.mit.edu/2019/mindfulness-mental-health-benefits-students-0826
6. Clemens C. Bauer et al., "Mindfulness Training Reduces Stress and Amygdala Reactivity to Fearful Faces in Middle-School Children," *American Psychological Association* 133, no. 6 (December 2019): 569–85, https://doi.org/10.1037/bne0000337
7. Britta K. Hölzel et al., "Mindfulness Practice Leads to Increases in Regional Brain Gray Matter Density," *Psychiatry Research: Neuroimaging* 191, no. 1 (January 2011): 36–43, https://doi.org/10.1016/j.pscychresns.2010.08.006
8. Christian Keysers and Valeria Gazzola, "Hebbian Learning and Predictive Mirror Neurons for Actions, Sensations and Emotions," *Philosophical Transactions of the Royal B* 369, no. 1644 (June 2014): 1–11, https://doi.org/10.1098/rstb.2013.0175
9. Carol Dweck, *Mindset: The New Psychology of Success* (New York: Ballantine Books, 2016).

Chapter Two

Building Community and Restorative Justice

What stood out in the circle was the way we were talking about real change in the world and also the way that we are evolving not only as people but as kind of a family who is always there for each other.

—Amani Lewis, high school student

To be compassionate is to feel deeply for another person as they experience the ups and downs associated with life.

—Aden Bachan Rigault, high school student

If you want to go quickly, go alone. If you want to go far, go together.

—African proverb

Building a strong class community takes right intention, patience, clearseeing, and—perhaps most important of all—good policies.

My own mindfulness class policies owe a gigantic debt to the Restorative Justice tradition, where I've learned structures to help make enlightened community real.

Restorative Justice is centered on meaningful, community-based conflict resolution; but the part of the tradition that has transformed my own teaching practice is about building strong, stable communities, and how the communities we create can become a source of empowerment and healing, even as we face the difficult challenges of systemic racism, generational trauma, and the many faces of oppression.

• • •

"No! That's absolutely *not* tolerated in here!" My co-teacher hollers as one student calls another stupid. The next day, the same thing happens. And again. Taking the kids into the hall one at a time and talking with them helps for a few days. Having a whole-class discussion about respect leads to a lot of teen eye-rolling but helps for a few days, too. But it's clearly not about the kids.

The real problem was that the class was a free-for-all, not that the kids didn't understand that bullying is bad. What was needed was infrastructure, not emphatic, emotional speeches.

People who are not teachers routinely express that you *must* have a zero-tolerance, no-bullying policy. Yes. But let's be real: if we get to the point that the students are bullying each other, we have failed to create the conditions for a well-functioning learning community.

One of my mentors would say, "You have to take responsibility for the fact that everything that happens in your classroom is the result of something you have created and reinforced." Period.

Pretty much every teacher knows firsthand what a train wreck looks like. We've all been there.

That's exactly why some teachers wield power so vehemently and learn to *punish* kids into learning instead of walking next to them on their *own* path. They want to avoid the train wrecks. They come to think it is the only way, that it is for the students' own good, and that if they don't rule with an iron fist, all hell will break loose.

To be fair, this is how many teachers were (and in some cases still are) trained.

But there is another way. Or, more precisely, there are multiple overlapping systems that interact to provide other ways.

The first systems we must attend to are curriculum, instruction, feedback, assessment, and grading. These systems must be clear, transparent, engaging, appropriately challenging, culturally aligned, and designed with the specific needs of our students in mind.

If these systems are not in place, there are no techniques that can build a stable and thriving classroom community. Instead, there will be chaos, and no one can be expected to be their best self in chaos.

In education, we are familiar with the idea of "creating community," but we would be well served to also consider the idea of "holding a container" or "holding space," language more typical of a yoga or mindfulness retreat center. In holding a container, we take responsibility for creating and sustaining a space of safety, communication, and inspiration—in other words the site of community.

In my mindfulness classes, I hold frequent Restorative Justice–style circle discussions to help us build a strong community.

There is a magic to a circle.

At the first circle, we discuss that Indigenous people from all over the world—including the Maori from New Zealand, and First Nations people of Canada and the United States—have gathered in circles throughout human history to build community, make decisions, and resolve conflict.

In the first circle discussion, we also read the "Seven Core Assumptions of Peacekeeping Circles" as a group. They are:

1. The true self in everyone is good, wise, and powerful;
2. The world is profoundly interconnected;
3. All human beings have a deep desire to be in a good relationship;
4. All humans have gifts and everyone is needed for what they bring;
5. Everything we need to make positive change is already here;
6. Human beings are holistic;
7. We need practices to build habits of living from the core self.[1]

Then, using these principles as a guide, each group cocreates class agreements.

Class agreements are not rules. They are guidelines we create and hold each other to so everyone can feel safe, seen, supported, and valued. Some past student examples include, "No judgment. All feelings are fine. Never give up on yourself. Speak loudly because what you say is important. It's OK to struggle sometimes. Don't talk over other people." They can even be aspirational, such as, "Treat each other how we want to be treated in order for us to all feel safe. Be a warrior of the heart. Don't contribute to oppression in any way."

The agreements we make together support us in making the world we want to live in. Before nearly every circle discussion, we revisit our class agreements. We go around the circle in real space, or down the list of participants in virtual space, and each student says what their top agreement is for today, and why they chose that particular agreement. They also have the option of changing or adding to our existing agreements.

To be honest, I never thought this would work. It seemed much too boring and repetitive. But thanks to Restorative Justice training, I implemented it as an experiment, and the integrity of my classroom communities noticeably improved.

Students at this age care deeply how they fit in and relate to the larger group. Also, creating the class agreements is, in itself, a community-building practice.

With one class, we spent two full class periods debating one single class agreement. At issue was whether or not sarcasm should be allowed in our community; and if yes, where the boundaries should be. I adjusted the instructional calendar to make time for this discussion since I wanted to do everything I could to support the students in taking the class agreements seriously; and since the discussion itself strengthened the community.

High school student Anahlia wrote, "In the circle, we were showing each other love and respect. The circle is a space, a place, where you trust people and tell them mostly anything."[2]

After a month or so, we have our agreements memorized, so when we visit them at the beginning of a circle it's a ritual, a symbol of the safe space we have created together—something most students take great pride in. Even shy-identified students are willing to share their top agreement, and it's a chance to hear everyone's voice on a low-stakes prompt. This also gives students an opportunity to speak on their personal values.

"One thing that stood out for me in the discussion circle was the fact that we all chose a similar line from the poem and we were able to connect to each other's ideas,"[3] one high school student shared.

The circle is really about seeing and being seen, and hearing and being heard, even more than anything we actually say. It's about how we are with each other, and how we are in community. It's *practicing* making the world we want to live in.

In real space, chairs or cushions are arranged in a circle. Any furniture that might make it tempting to hide behind other participants is removed, setting up good conditions. There is also a circle centerpiece of some sort, ideally with objects that are meaningful to the group.

Occasionally, we open the discussion to volunteers (especially helpful at the end of a round), but most often we go patiently around the circle one round at a time, allowing each participant a chance to respond to a given prompt in their own way. In a remote environment, the circle facilitator goes patiently down the participant list, inviting each student to speak when it is their turn.

To hold space well, facilitators have to do a lot of quiet management. This includes designing engaging and inclusive activities, selecting anchor texts, paraphrasing, acknowledging students' feelings, knowing when sharing something themselves will support the discussion, providing strategic prompts that build toward deepening understanding, managing time, and redirecting the flow when necessary.

I'm from a big, rowdy family where everyone talks at once and you have to be loud to get your point across. Being in a circle is a totally different way of relating. I'm not sure if a one-time observer would even be able to see what's really happening, but student feedback is clear. They are proud of their role in creating a truly respectful space, and interested in their classmates' opinions and stories. In the words of high school student Hannah Medor and countless others, "It really helped me to know that I am not alone."[4]

In my first Restorative Justice training, I spent a lot of the week crying. It was so moving to listen deeply and to speak my truth. It seems like such a simple format, but it can be very powerful.

Once in a great while, I have to say something like, "Dear one, we don't talk like that here. I know you're just kidding, and so-and-so isn't offended by what you're saying at all, but that's not the way we act with each other here. Here we're making the world we want to live in."

I used to get occasional pushback to the effect of, "Miss! You just don't understand how we are! That's just how we play with each other." But I haven't heard that one in years. I hope it's because the world is improving. Or maybe it's because I've done my job to make being a willing participant in a loving community the most obvious and appealing choice.

The foundation of love, support, and respect that we build in circle discussions carries over into the other days of the week.

Even if circle discussions aren't a frequent feature of your class, you can start the year by cocreating class agreements, and revisiting them according to a regular, set routine. Once all class groups have made agreements, I make a version that incorporates everyone's so I can post them in the classroom. In a remote environment, we keep a separate set of class agreements for each group, since physical wall space isn't an issue.

Building community is about creating the conditions for strong relationships to grow.

Early in the year, we do a unit on Mindful Communication with an emphasis on listening. Students use these skills in circle discussions, class discussions, and in their independent relationships. It also makes the idea of building a strong community more concrete.

We also do a partnered speaking-and-listening practice. Before pairing students up, I tell them in advance who their partner will be, drawing some students to the side to tell them privately if I think there is any chance of pushback so no one will feel rejected. If a student is adamant about not working with someone, I accommodate the request, taking care to not let the other student know.

In each pair, I ask one person to raise their hand, and say, "OK, you will be the listener first. Your job is to stay totally silent, to just be there for the speaker, and let them know you're listening. Your job is also to notice if your attention drifts away, and gently bring it back to the speaker. This time, the way we are listening *is* our meditation. Instead of bringing your attention back to the breath or whatever you were paying attention to, you keep bringing your attention back to the speaker, and noticing what's happening for you if you're not listening to them."

Then we do a brief period of breath-centered practice, and when the bell rings again the speaker begins to speak. I usually give two minutes for this, but it can vary depending on what's happening in the room. I also move around, supporting people who are having a tough time getting started, in some cases even giving students their lines. Next we pause, debrief, go back into silent practice, and then change roles.

Some important questions to ask in debriefing are: Did you find it difficult to stay quiet and listen? Did you find it easy? Did you find that it was hard to stay focused on what the speaker was saying? For the speakers, did anyone feel like their listener was really *there* for them? Did this feel different than how we usually listen to each other?

If we're lucky, someone will share that they really bonded, and we can ask follow-up questions about their experience to refine everyone's understanding. If someone says they noticed their mind wandered a lot or that they zoned out a lot, we would do well to praise them for tracking themselves so well, and emphasize that we've accidentally trained our brains to bounce around like crazy, and that noticing what's happening will help us learn to keep our focus stronger in the future. We can also let them know it's a normal experience, and part of the growth process we are going through.

We usually practice this twice in a row the first time, leaving a lot of time to debrief and reset. After the second round, I also ask what other skills we've learned that can support us in being good listeners. I have posters in the classroom that we keep adding to with skills and techniques we've learned that we can reference for these questions.

It's important to have a compelling prompt in order for this to work. When I'm first teaching this practice, I invite students to tell the story of their name, using the same prompts from the Name Story activity that are listed in the chapter on representation. I also provide the support of having the prompts visible in the front of the classroom; and I always model it with one student (who agreed in advance) before putting it to the group.

Being clear about timing is important for this to work. It's also important to emphasize that only one person is speaking. The other one is just listening. For many, this will feel counterintuitive and awkward, but just reassure them that we're testing it out as an experiment to see what info we can find about ourselves. If they run out of things to say, they can repeat what they already said or just sit quietly until the bell rings again.

Usually students appreciate time to talk informally after the formal practice concludes. On many occasions, students form a bond during this exercise, and it is not uncommon for there to be tears. Once this practice is part of our class culture, we visit it over the course of the year, especially when we are addressing deeper topics like difficult emotions, forgiveness, and empathy.

It can be very moving to feel truly seen, a rare gift in a world carried away with its insistence on speed and constant entertainment.

This practice works best in real space. It is difficult to adapt to a remote environment because it requires extensive facilitation even within the partnerships.

Students are also trained to facilitate small groups, a strategy for student leadership that works well both in real and remote space. The most extroverted and confident students are the first leaders, but once they get comfortable, they help to train the next tier of facilitators, until everyone has had the opportunity to test out what it feels like to lead. In these cases, it's also very important to have clear prompts and tasks for students to accomplish. Just telling them to discuss something and sending them on their way has never worked for my groups. I typically arrange with students in advance so they know if they'll be called on to lead, and provide them with the materials beforehand. This allows everyone to take ownership of the class and to practice taking on new roles, in some cases expanding beyond what they thought they were capable of.

Considerations for Building Community

- Instruction, feedback, and assessment are clear, transparent, and engaging
- Space is held as safely as possible
- Class agreements are collaboratively generated
- Regular circle discussions are held
- Mindful communication skills are explicitly taught
- There are many opportunities for collaboration
- There are many opportunities for student leadership
- Students facilitate small groups and some lessons
- Student voice is elevated
- Representation is diverse and reflects students' identities

It is always important to create the conditions for inclusivity, and to be constantly analyzing our systems for ways they can be more inclusive. Either *everyone* feels included, or it's not inclusive.

Creating opportunities for student leadership and student voice are also essential. These supports are discussed in detail in the chapter "Elevating Student Voice and Leadership."

If I'm picking up on something, or suspect that a student is being subtly left out but I'm not sure about hidden dynamics, I ask students privately what's going on. Sometimes I find out about old grudges, recent fights in a different class, or other factors. In these cases, it takes skillful balancing to sustain the community while supporting and encouraging students to work through differences. I avoid telling them if I think they're wrong or right, or giving any advice, and instead ask questions, reflect and acknowledge feelings, and let them know that I'm confident they have the skills to work it out. In rare cases, students need to seek mediation with a school leader before the conflict can be fully resolved.

Being skillful and intentional with representation also builds community, and helps make a space where students feel seen and included. Supports and considerations for inclusive representation are discussed in detail in the chapter "Why Nuanced Representation Matters in Mindfulness Classrooms and Beyond."

Working together to build a strong class community is not only a condition needed for individual learning and transformation but is itself a teaching, and one that is well worth the effort.

NOTES

1. "Free Stuff," Living Justice Press, nonprofit publisher for restorative justice since 2002, February 13, 2023, https://livingjusticepress.org/free-stuff/

2. Anahlia, student comment in written classwork, 2021. Name changed for anonymity.

3. Student comment in written classwork, 2022. Name changed for anonymity.

4. Hannah Medor, student comment in written classwork, 2020.

Chapter Three

Why Nuanced Representation Matters in Mindfulness Classrooms and Beyond

> When practicing mindfulness, your inner self grows more stable and stronger, allowing for you to understand yourself better.
>
> —Bryan Cepeda, high school student

> More than anything, culture creates a sense of belonging—and belonging makes our bodies feel safe. This is why culture matters to us so deeply.
>
> —Resmaa Menakem, trauma specialist and author of *My Grandmother's Hands: Racialized Trauma and the Pathway to Mending Our Hearts and Bodies*

"I see you there; and I am grateful for it." In the book *True Love* Zen meditation teacher Thich Nhat Hahn shares his personal practice of saying this phrase inside his head while intending to truly *see* another person.[1]

Representation matters.

Responsible, nuanced representation impacts students on conscious and unconscious levels and lays a foundation for trust in mindfulness classrooms and beyond.

It is essential to provide rich, meaningful representations and to center a broad range of narratives so everyone has a chance to see themselves reflected in the room. We don't need to automatically reject materials if they meet the needs of our students just because they feature white people, but we do need to go to lengths to make sure representation is balanced. Thus, people of color are just as likely, if not more likely, to be the face of mindfulness as anyone else.

It's also important to include people who identify as members of LGBTQIA+ and disability communities and to encourage and model inclusive language.

In addition, we can strive to create a physical environment where students can be themselves. Ideally, creating a site that encourages honest conversation, crying, connecting, hugging, digging deep, dancing, supporting each other, speaking our truths, and taking risks might involve making significant adjustments to a traditional classroom, and getting input from students and families about what would be most inspiring and supportive.

We can also feature quotes and images of our students themselves and of people they are likely to identify with in the physical space.

To create an opportunity for students to express personal and cultural identity right from the beginning, I start with a unit on identity that includes a "Name Story" artwork, wherein students can write, draw, and collage on the subject of their own name, responding to any of the following prompts:

- What is your name?
- Do you have a nickname?
- How did you get your name?
- Are you named after anyone?
- Is your name (or the spelling of your name) unique?
- Is your name common in a certain culture?
- What does your name make you think of?
- Do you like your name?
- Would you ever want to change your name?
- What does your name mean to you?

Then, in a circle discussion, each person has a chance to share their story with a partner and then with the full group.

Regularly held Restorative Justice–style circle discussions are an opportunity to build community and practice seeing and hearing each other. The job of the teacher/facilitator is to set the conditions and gently insist on the right of each student to share their experiences without being questioned or having to defend their validity.

No one should ever have to worry that another member of the community (especially not the teacher) will minimize, make light of, impose a positive spin, hijack for their own purposes, or otherwise disrespect what is shared within the container of the classroom.

Training in facilitation and continually working to be sensitive to racist, sexist, anti-LGBTQIA+, and ableist narratives, including knowing how to skillfully redirect conversation to protect vulnerable participants while triggering a minimum of guilt or shame, is part of representation, too.

These are essential skills in any classroom, but are, again, even more essential in a mindfulness classroom, where students may be especially vulnerable.

Even if we celebrate diversity, it's important to consider what we're centering as the unquestioned norm.

What is centered as the norm becomes the ruler by which everyone is measured.

The power to define the norm is often guarded by dominant groups who have an interest in sustaining their own position as the center of what is standard. This is part of the complex machinery of white supremacy.

We have to make narratives about white-dominant norms visible in order to dismantle them. We also have to provide counternarratives through every means available: language, music, images, texts, and the experts we reference and include in our curriculum materials.

Providing rich, meaningful representations, and taking turns centering a broad range of narratives so everyone has a chance to see themselves reflected in the room, is essential if students are to trust their teacher and feel safe and inspired to take risks. Deep learning will simply not be available otherwise.

Cultural appropriation—inappropriately and disrespectfully taking on the customs or practices of another group, especially when enacted by a dominant group—is a risk when we strive for diverse representations that acknowledge and elevate as many voices as possible. It is important to educate ourselves and to be constantly evaluating our offerings through this lens, but this risk should not lock us into fearing to represent groups other than the ones we personally identify with. We *all* need to feel like we belong.

This is true in every classroom but is even more important in mindfulness classrooms where, if the conditions are carefully orchestrated, students may start to look deep inside, to see their own stories, to reckon with their experiences, to heal themselves from trauma, and, ideally, to find greater access to hope, including both personal and collective aspiration.

Another way to understand the significance of what we center as the norm concerns gender.

When we're forthright about gender pronouns, we make space for each other. That way, if someone's pronouns don't conform to someone else's expectations, *they* aren't automatically the "weirdo." Because we've all made our pronouns explicit, we haven't centered cisgender as the unquestioned, unexamined norm.

In the same way, it's important to make whiteness explicit, so it's no longer the assumed norm. Getting to be the assumed norm—the gold standard by which everyone else is measured—is a manifestation of white privilege. In the words of author and antiracist activist Ibram X. Kendi, "Whoever creates the cultural standard usually puts themself at the top of the hierarchy."[2]

To describe a teacher, we might say, "The white lady who's always wearing high heels." We could include whiteness in a story character's description. If we are white, we can make our own whiteness explicit. We have to stop thinking it's impolite to describe someone as white. This is part of "white fragility"[3] and it is really just a way to try to keep race off the table, to avoid examining the systems we're immersed in, and to avoid taking personal responsibility.

In order to enact meaningful, inclusive representation, teachers must also be willing to be challenged and even triggered without trying to reestablish their own narratives, and must guard against minimizing or squashing narratives that challenge their identity or sense of what they believe should be valued.

In a classroom, we can't hear every single thing, but we can make sure everyone understands that how someone feels is not negotiable. Period.

After the death of George Floyd, a Black man who was brutally murdered by a police officer in 2020, I held circle discussions for students to process their feelings. I was teaching ninth grade students, and we had recently shifted into remote learning because of the pandemic. Thankfully, when this crisis fully emerged (it had already been going on for centuries), we already had strong relationships to build on. Even so, especially as a white person, I

Considerations for Skillful Representation

- Meaningful, diverse representations are provided
- A broad range of narratives are centered
- Quotes and images by the students themselves are featured
- Activities that explore and celebrate identity are included
- Teachers are trained in skillful facilitation
- Whiteness is just as explicit as any other identity
- Emotions and experiences are validated
- Diverse experts are referenced and highlighted

felt totally inept. But I did my best to hold space with integrity and to avoid causing harm. In the words of high school student Deborah Eustache, "When I saw that video, it was like it was *me*."[4]

For white educators, being willing to hear the full force of every person's truth without flinching is part of taking responsibility for white privilege and witnessing its impacts.

For all educators, being willing to witness each student's truth is a way of taking responsibility for our children and committing ourselves to the collective process of reckoning.

As teachers, we're trained to solve problems. We're trained to fix. And we don't *want* to feel all of this. But when it comes to trauma, including trauma caused by racism, sometimes the most powerful thing we can do is witness—even if it means we have to be with grave discomfort; even if in witnessing a child's experience, we are forced to confront our own.

In this way, children come to know that how they feel isn't crazy or weird or abnormal but an understandable response to their lived experiences. By sitting with their feelings, students begin to shift their internal landscapes and heal themselves. Being emotionally grounded and holding students with spaciousness and acceptance can support their process of self-healing.

As teachers, this is how we become truly trustworthy.

We have no control over how each student will encounter their own path. All we can do is make the conditions and try to avoid causing harm. Then the magic takes over, and our role is to step back and witness the students in healing themselves and each other.

NOTES

1. Thich Nhat Hanh, *True Love: A Practice for Awakening the Heart* (Boulder: Shambhala, 2006).
2. Ibram X. Kendi, *How to Be an Antiracist* (New York: One World, 2019).
3. Robin DiAngelo, *White Fragility* (New York: Public Science, 2016).
4. Deborah Eustache, student comment in written classwork, 2020.

Chapter Four

Instruction

It's OK to accept the good and the bad, but you have to learn to look at things differently, not always black and white, life happens in the gray too.

—Mea Richards, high school student

Good instruction makes students accountable for their own learning and makes learning a process of empowerment, never one of compliance.

Good intentions alone are not enough.

Excellence in teaching does require good intentions, but also excellent systems, and ongoing examination of the personal and cultural narratives that impact perspectives and choices.

Excellent instruction is constantly evolving, as new strategies are created and tested over time. Teachers sometimes express fatigue at the constant influx of new strategies and systems, but it is essential to continue to experiment with new ideas, slowly sculpting our systems so they are constantly being refined, examined, and further refined.

The strategies themselves are important, but just as important is the mindset of curiosity and receptivity to new ideas.

I'm going to describe my current understanding of excellent instruction, but please know that this will (and should) be constantly updated.

When I was in school for teaching, I was trained in something called strategy instruction. As a teaching lab, I had to work with one student for an entire semester.

I worked with a tenth grader who had a second grade reading level. I had to select two learning targets in response to the student's needs, and design lessons to move her toward those targets. I chose a vocabulary goal and a goal around the skill of inferencing. During our one semester together, my student went from a second grade reading level to a fifth grade reading level—a remarkable jump. I learned that targeted, considered instruction really works.

During my first year of teaching, I also taught at a school where they used outcomes-based assessment—meaning the grades were based entirely on a student's ability to master selected skills—though they were still figuring out exactly what that would look like. I particularly keyed into the idea that we had to find a way to teach students even if they had low attendance, and that attendance could not be factored into grading.

I took these experiences with me, and at my next school, in response to the needs of the students, proposed a vocabulary class that would have specific language-learning targets, using poetry, spoken word, and rap as a doorway in. This seemed to some like a foolish thing to do, since no one had yet been able to design a stand-alone vocabulary intervention that worked. But there were some modest gains.

That same year, I struggled with a co-teacher who used fury to make up for poor instruction. She was tiny, but when students weren't listening to her, she would take a wooden yard stick and slap it full force on the desk of the offending students, causing them to jump, pull their shoulders quickly to their ears, and hold their hands up in front of their faces to protect themselves. She picked great texts, but we more or less bobbed along with no goals to guide us, just the general idea that reading and comprehension questions would do some good.

I really struggled in this classroom. I felt like I was constantly trying to build kids back up from abuse, and to angle and create conditions to mitigate it. I didn't feel like I could be myself at all, and I had many nights of poor sleep.

At the end of our second year of partnership, I retooled one of our units so it matched my vision of how things should be. At my insistence, she had put away the yard stick, but grading was still almost entirely based on whether or not students did the work—compliance—rather than progress on specific skills. I wanted to give kids more agency and to create a system that was more transparent so the students really understood what was expected, what they needed to do, and why they needed to do it.

I looked carefully at our standards, then designed a set of learning goals that would be measurable steps toward these standards. Next I looked at the calendar so I knew exactly how many days we had to work with and carefully designed each day. I made sure that for every one of the learning goals—I think there were twelve in this first unit—there was at least one aligned assessment (and ideally several consecutive assessments), so by the end we would have data to show we had accomplished every one of our learning targets and therefore our standards, and we could measure progress on each standard. I wrote a learning target, or aim, and agenda for each day, and created a column where I could write each day's assessment, along with the learning goal it aligned with. That way I could cross-check over the entire unit and make sure I hadn't left any learning goals out and that we had a way to assess everything.

I also planned to base the grade on whether or not the students had achieved each of these goals (though I still had a long way to go before I had a clear, efficient system for this).

I showed the unit to my then-principal and a storm cloud passed over her face. "She's going to freak out when she sees this," the principal said of my co-teacher.

I thought long and hard about what the threat was, what was likely to make my co-teacher freak out. I think it was, I think it *is*, really about power. This was over a decade ago and there has been some progress, but there are still teachers who think *they* are the ones controlling the learning—they are the authority, they are the source of the learning—and that students should be graded for being in class, following their instructions compliantly, and completing all tasks, no matter how random or inane.

And, as my then-principal predicted, my co-teacher did freak out when I presented the unit to her.

If I remember correctly, she flat out refused to teach with me ever again; and I was switched to a different co-teacher. Thankfully, my next co-teacher was exceptional, and was undergoing a transformation analogous to my own.

There is a name for this now. I guess the outcomes-based instruction that I had been exposed to at my first school was in the same family, but it was not yet widespread or well understood.

It's now called mastery-based (or outcomes-based or standards-based) instruction, assessment, and grading. Another strongly related concept is explicit instruction.

Many districts now have mandates to shift to mastery-based systems, but it is taking a long time for schools to fully understand and implement what must necessarily be called a paradigm shift.

Schools went along using basically the same format since the industrial revolution, which was designed to more or less brainwash new workers to make the country's products, until this option finally started to find its way to our systems.

The basic idea is that you start out with very clear goals, you communicate them to kids, you articulate the path to attaining those goals, and you assess kids constantly and provide feedback they can use to improve. Then you provide opportunities for kids to apply the feedback, and do the same thing again until they learn the skill or competency.

One teacher I know simply shifted to mastery-based grading codes instead of number or letter grades but otherwise kept doing exactly the same thing she'd been doing all along—politely but harshly demanding compliance and hoping for the best. Then she would talk about how "these kids" had to be ruled with an iron fist.

For years, I only called this "racism" at my own table over a bottle of wine with trusted friends. It felt impossible to call out what I saw and I had a hard time even finding language for it. I was in the principal's office with an angry co-teacher more times than I care to count.

I felt alienated, isolated, depressed, and crazy a lot of the time.

I'm not proud of it, but there have been times that I, myself, have resorted to demanding compliance—punishing kids to learn. The poorer my instructional systems, the more likely I have been to resort to punishing to learn.

Somewhat intuitively, I came around to a system that looks a lot like mastery-based grading as a result of careful observation of what worked. It was also based on analysis of what damaged my spirit and appeared to damage the spirits of students.

A lot of what motivated me was that demanding compliance made me miserable. And though students might have been acquiring skills, I knew I was doing more harm than good. Either I had to find a better way, or I would have to leave teaching.

When I finally shifted from sharing classrooms as a special education co-teacher in English classes to teaching independent mindfulness classes, I had some good models, and also a lot of examples of what *not* to do. Yet it remained to be seen if I could actually create a valid construct that matched my values. I also knew that if I tried to use punitive systems—by that I mostly mean demanding compliance and using harsh grading that's not well-aligned to standards, and possibly shaming, criticism, passive aggression, sarcasm, or harsh words—it would destroy the benefits of mindfulness and make me into a gigantic hypocrite.

I got to work. And it *is* a lot of work. You can't just show up and go along for the ride. Good instruction is a very sophisticated skill set.

I had to create my own curriculum because there wasn't one that would meet the unique needs of my students. I also had to create instructional systems that would hold us as a strong community, would be student-centered, would get students interested and keep them engaged, and would keep us meaningfully attentive to the course standards. On top of all that, I had to figure out how to involve families as learning partners, and how to build in accountability for students without resorting to punishment.

I started by designing standards. I based these on the New York State Social Emotional Learning Benchmarks,[1] the CASEL Core Competencies framework,[2] and student input. In the first semester, there were six standards, but they have since expanded to twelve (see appendix).

I then created a series of topics, or units, aligned to those standards. I did everything I could to get the most important ideas of that topic to stand up in memory. I created a booklet for each topic, an essential question, a related quote, diverse images that aligned with the topic, the standard we would focus on, key vocabulary words, daily lessons that included learning targets and checklists, and extension activities for students who completed classwork faster than the rest of the group.

Students would work their way through this booklet during the course of the week in our daily lessons. I graded them on Friday afternoons (and often into the weekend) and handed them back on Monday morning.

I worked very hard to make lessons multimodal, engaging, and to include diverse representations and references.

On top of that, I learned that lessons needed to be both pithy and aligned, and that I also had to weave in additional strands like vocabulary and actual mindfulness practice.

And on top of that, lessons had to be scaffolded enough so students who were absent could accomplish them on their own, and students with disabilities and English language learners could access them; but at the same time, they could not be redundant or padded with busy work, and they needed to be challenging enough for advanced learners.

Another consideration is that lessons within a unit or topic need to be appropriately sequenced so they spiral into deeper understanding.

None of this is easy.

In my class, there was also a checklist in the weekly booklet with every one of the week's tasks. Every task that was aligned to a standard would get its own grade. At this point, I was still shifting into fully mastery-based grading, and students would also receive a "weekly grade." The weekly grade was an accumulation of points for whether or not the student had completed all tasks for the week. This was definitely a compliance grade, though it only accounted for 10 percent of the overall class grade.

Since then, I've eliminated compliance-based grading entirely, but it was a long process to develop the new systems necessary to support this shift.

Instead of assigning grading categories of "classwork, homework, projects, tests, and participation," I aligned my grading categories with course standards for a given marking period. So my grading categories might be "Emotion Regulation, Responsible Decision Making, and Self Awareness," which are three of my standards. This allowed me to track progress on a given standard, and to easily communicate progress to students and families. Using more general grading categories left things too murky and didn't support the transparency and agency I needed to build into my system.

I am particularly likely to hiss and narrow my eyes when teachers use "participation points." Participation points can be totally vague and up to a teacher's subjective (possibly racist) discretion. Participation points also allow teachers to play favorites, to pad the grades of compliant students even if they are not mastering the standards, and they provide an officially sanctioned, structurally embedded way to punish students for noncompliance. Even worse, participation points let teachers off the hook—instead of creating and articulating standards, daily learning targets, and aligned assessments on which to base valid grading, teachers can use squishy, vague criteria that have nothing to do with achievement.

This is oppression in action—systems that reward children for complying with authority and punish them for noncompliance fail to empower them. Instead, they are forced to choose either to comply with power structures that do not align with their best interests and submit to learning or to *not* comply and be denied access to education. This may be especially problematic for children of color, who may understandably experience compliance, ipso facto, as acquiescing to a racist system.

In a just system, compliance and learning must not be conjoined.

We must create conditions where learning can happen whether students are compliant or not, and where students are encouraged to push back, to think critically, and to evaluate teachings in terms of how they relate to their own needs and experiences.

This is not easy, either.

There are many ways that mastery-based grading goes wrong. Some boil mastery-based instruction, grading, and assessment down to the idea that if students can master the learning targets and standards, and can demonstrate them through any form of assessment, they should get a high grade. So in effect, a student might do nothing for an entire semester, then do a project at the end and theoretically demonstrate mastery.

The trick is that you have to design curriculum and instruction with enough rigor so that it needs to be done sequentially and methodically in order to be accomplished. Students shouldn't be able to pull it off in a couple of google searches. We also need to design projects with clear outcomes, and if we intend for a project to assess multiple standards, it needs to be extremely well-designed and segmented.

Overvaluing performance-based assessment projects, or PBAs, can lead to a similar pit of quicksand, as the emphasis is on the *thing,* the project, rather than on the accumulation and deepening of specific, measurable skills.

If word gets around that your class is a joke and that you can just do the final project to pass, forget about garnering meaningful engagement.

All too often, mastery-based grading is mistaken for vague, mooshy teaching. With mastery-based instruction, teaching is strategic, precise, and rigorous, and accountability is essential. In fact, accountability is built in with regular protocols and routines. Accountability is balanced with frequent and specific feedback, praise, and strong relationships with students and families, but it is definitely *not* just a wild free-for-all.

The shift into remote learning at the start of the COVID-19 pandemic was traumatic for both students and teachers. One day we were sitting in circle discussions, eating bad pizza in the cafeteria and making group posters, and the next the school was dark and we were all reeling, wondering what had just happened.

I never would have wished it on any of us, but as a result of this challenge, I developed a whole new skill set that I never would have otherwise unlocked. In some ways, I can't believe the teacher I was before the pandemic. Despite knowing better, I still occasionally resorted to punitive practices when things weren't going my way. Since the start of remote learning, I worked hard to create strong systems and build relationships to keep students engaged. Although there was no penalty for not attending zoom classes, and the assignments were carefully scaffolded so students could accomplish them on their own, I had 85–90 percent attendance even during the remote learning period.

Although I used to grade student booklets once a week, in remote learning I learned I had to grade work before every class meeting, and use quotes from the students' work on the previous day to help drive instruction. This daily assessment, feedback, and grading helped keep me closely attentive to students' progress, misconceptions, and needs; and I continued this practice of daily grading even following the remote period.

I also tinkered a lot so the layout of the remote classroom was straightforward and easy to access, so even if, for example, your family members all got COVID and you didn't join classes for three weeks, you could pick right back up without needing a long introduction. Even back to in-person classes, I have continued to use a similar format and to keep my remote classroom current and tidy, even when most of the work is happening in person and on paper.

On the remote site, I include a resources section, which contains class agreements, remote link, teacher contact information, school counselors' contact information, the course syllabus, practice instructions, a script for leading mindfulness practice, the school bell schedule, steps for what to do if you are ever triggered during practice, and any other information that students might need to access regularly.

Attributes of Skillful Instruction

- Teachers are constantly refining strategies
- Learning outcomes and daily goals are clearly defined
- Learning tasks are clearly defined
- Assessment and feedback are consistent and specific
- Students have agency and are supported in working toward learning goals
- Learning relies on agency and engagement, not compliance
- Instruction is multimodal, culturally responsive, antiracist, scaffolded, rigorous, and tailored
- Friction for achieving daily goals is reduced or eliminated

The classwork section is broken up by topics, with the newest at the top, and each topic is broken up by days. Every day there is an assignment. For each assignment, all information is included in one document, even if I have to insert images and links, since I noticed that whenever there was more than one attachment for an assignment, less work was handed in.

This is an example of eliminating friction—any obstacle to ease of use—and I continue to evaluate practices with the lens of how I can reduce friction so students can focus on the day's learning target.

In response to student feedback, I've also made the student lessons more friendly, with bright colors, blocked sections, student-friendly fonts, fun images, and sentence starters in a bright, recognizable color and signature font to key students in to where they have to respond in writing.

Instead of shoring up and deepening the harms of oppression, mastery-based instruction, assessment, and grading encourages teachers to up their game and entices students to buy in. Once they know what they are learning and why they are learning it, and that they are the ones driving the process, they understand that the learning is for *them,* not to appease a teacher, and not to avoid punishment.

Once we have well-functioning instructional systems and strong classroom communities, they will hold us. Then we can relax, be present, and follow our embodied intuition to understand our own needs and the needs of our students. We can notice when a child who is normally withdrawn starts to shine. We can provide emotional support when it's needed. We can support kids in developing leadership skills and then hand the reins over. We can share jokes. We can be ourselves. We can actually *love* our jobs. This is all very much possible.

In fact, this is all very much necessary.

NOTES

1. "New York State Social Emotional Learning Benchmarks," NYSED, accessed August 6, 2023, htttps://www.p12.nysed.gov/sss/sel.html

2. "What Is the CASEL Framework?," CASEL, accessed March 3, 2023, https://casel.org/fundamentals-of-sel/what-is-the-casel-framework/

Chapter Five

Making It Engaging

Mindfulness is beneficial because it helps you have better peace of mind and clarity and it can help you develop a routine for yourself to keep you motivated and energetic.

—Nia Gomez, high school student

We must remember that our students are innately creative, innovative, and collaborative, and that we suppress these things with our control. Empowerment is the key that will unlock them.

—Kevin Parr, teacher

There are shredded-up magazine pages covering every inch of the rug and all horizontal surfaces in the mindfulness studio. There are also glue guns, glue sticks, scissors, markers, and collage materials strewn about. A student is sitting at the teacher's desk, helping other students print images they want for their vision boards. She's also DJing from the class playlist. Two students are dancing by one of the big conference tables while cutting out images for their vision boards. Even for me, who tends to thrive in a cheerfully chaotic environment, this place is a wreck.

This is the first time we're creating vision boards as part of the curriculum. It's part of a topic called Visualization, Goal Setting, and the Power of Intention.

On this day, half the students decide to stay on throughout lunch period and continue to work on their creations.

The studio is beautiful, with rugs covering most of the floor, a row of comfortable barrel-back chairs, gold and red details and sculptures, a row of chic designer tables that once lived at an upscale architectural firm, red meditation cushions spaced out over the expanse of rugs, and a tabletop waterfall in front of the classroom.

Early each semester, we create a vibrant word wall for vocabulary words that relate to emotions. The panels are made with bright paper, markers, and glittering collage materials.

A beautiful space helps students want to be in it, especially if it seems different from the rest of the school. And it definitely helps with branding—ongoing attention to making the program seem desirable and compelling from the perspective of teenagers and school leaders.

In mindfulness class, we don't just sit around meditating all the time. The curriculum includes a long list of social and emotional skills and concepts that are readily coupled with mindfulness, including how to achieve states of flow, dealing with difficult emotions, responsible decision making, empathy, and healthy relationships.

To make it engaging, we mix it up, including art, poetry, drawing, acting, analyzing anchor texts, games, videos, making posters, writing, discussion, and movement.

Of course, we always balance the need for compelling novelty with clear, powerful infrastructure and protocols so the overall framework remains predictable and feels manageable even for students who don't attend every day.

There are many evidence-based strategies teachers can use to encourage engagement. None of these are new, but the following are some strategies that seem to work particularly well in a mindfulness classroom.

As most teachers know, it's helpful to set up many opportunities for collaboration. When we're working on a text, students can work in groups with specific roles to create posters or otherwise present what they've gathered from the reading. Another way students collaborate is by using a jigsaw—dividing up questions, then sharing their answers with each other and summarizing key points.

Setting up appealing challenges before students apply themselves to a text can also be helpful. For example, "This poem is about a hole in the sidewalk, but come on, we all know it's not *really* about a hole in the sidewalk, right? What I want to know is if you can figure out the *metaphor* meaning of the poem, like what it's *really* about, on a deep level."

Providing student choice is another well-documented way to increase engagement. Allowing students to choose the format of assessments, to select from a list of questions, and to choose different options for projects, among many others, can be very helpful.

Taking a class outside or to a different site in the building and planning frequent field trips can help keep things lively, too.

Of course, one of the most important strategies for engaging students is to present rich, meaningful representations of people who look like our students. It is much easier to see ourselves succeeding at anything if we have examples of people who look like us succeeding at it.

Also, music can be a doorway, and is an area where most kids are experts and are happy to share their knowledge. Having students DJ, suggest songs, and collaborate on a class playlist helps make a joyful, inviting space.

Another important bucket of engagement strategies is to create endless opportunities for leadership. Teachers need to *really* know that we are not the ultimate authority. We are rarely teaching students anything they don't already know or can't learn from the internet. We're mostly just holding space, and helping them to be intentional about what they already understand intuitively.

There are many ways to create student leadership in a mindfulness classroom. One is to support students in learning to lead meditations, then having them lead at the beginning of class or for schoolwide events. Another way is to create student leadership programs, where students from previous years assist in the classroom with younger students. Yet another is to create consultation committees, which give students the opportunity to have meaningful input on the development of course curriculum and protocols.

Students can also facilitate small groups, including breakout groups in a remote environment. To do this, we can provide explicit instruction in facilitation, then create opportunities for students to lead. If some still feel too shy, we can assign a co-facilitator to help out or join groups ourselves when a student is new to facilitating; and we can provide many opportunities to debrief and build skills.

The students will teach us every second. We need to follow their lead. Seriously. We can be on the lookout for new insights that the kids lead us to, and trumpet those. Occasionally we need to debunk misconceptions, but only very gently, helping them to uncover misconceptions on their own whenever possible, and working hard behind the scenes to make that happen. Often we can do that simply by emphasizing a more skillful perspective, without even having to directly address a misconception, or can offer anonymous group suggestions about ideas that have come up that we want to ask questions about or gently push back on.

Once, I shifted my attention from one student to call on another too quickly. "Hey, you missed the point of what I said," he called out loudly. "You just skimmed it over. That's fine. It doesn't really matter." He hunched his shoulders, looked down, and bent forward. The entire room was silent, possibly wondering if I would come down on him for calling me out. I took a breath, trying to read the situation. "Thank you for letting me know that I got it wrong, and that I wasn't really paying attention," I said. "That took a lot of courage for you to call me out, and I appreciate it. I care about how you feel, and I'm glad you shared this. Are you willing to resay your point, so I can listen more carefully this time?" The room relaxed. This was a turning point for buy-in with this group; and I realized that being receptive and supporting students when they do push back or call me out can be an intentional strategy to improve trust and buy-in.

Another strategy to support student engagement is taking every opportunity to highlight and celebrate successes in family communications. This could be that a student stepped up as a leader, supported a classmate, shared a key insight that opened up a discussion, did an outstanding job on classwork, completed daily classwork for the first time, did a great job leading a meditation, made a particularly moving comment, or that they brought a new perspective we hadn't previously considered.

In fact, any time a student does something we want to encourage, we can highlight it. If a student who does not verbally participate often says something in class, we can send a message to families to sing their praises. If a student who rarely submits work does hand work in, we can try to find something exemplary in what they wrote to share with the whole class the next day. If a student who typically talks a mile a minute pauses to invite a peer to share, we can praise them publicly for pausing to make space for a friend, and reach out to their families with praise. Some kids are always willing to share their thoughts in discussion, so we can reach out to express gratitude for their willingness to help the class by sharing their insights. Every time a kid extends themselves beyond what they were previously willing or able to deliver, we can go all out to reinforce it.

This helps students feel seen and valued, builds buy-in, and encourages them to do the work. Going all out to praise, support, and encourage small steps toward progress is exponentially more effective than trying to correct behaviors we find less productive.

That is not to say that there isn't a place for accountability. By all means, accountability—especially when clear, manageable objectives and tasks have been laid out and then are ignored or completed half-assed—is crucial and supports meaningful engagement. If students don't meet daily learning targets, it is important to reflect that in assessment, provide feedback, conference with them, and sometimes conference with families.

But if you have worked all along to lay down a clear path, to support students, to share information on what they are learning with families, and to sing students' praises, accountability will feel like just a normal part of the ongoing process, not a way to shame or punish or as an indictment of a student's or a family's character.

Centering student voice, discussed at length in the chapter "Elevating Student Voice and Leadership," especially quoting and amplifying the actual words of our students, is also very important.

Centering student voice also involves creating a strong community where students feel safe in sharing their thoughts, where they have meaningful opportunities to engage with relevant, rigorous ideas and prompts, and where they feel inspired to make connections to their own experiences, share their thoughts with peers, and integrate new concepts through discussion and reflection.

In addition to all of the other roles that a teacher has to fulfill, part of our job is to inspire. It's important for us to step back from the spotlight and hand the mic over to kids often, but occasionally it can be helpful to step up with dramatic, thematic stories and even with carefully designed speeches to inspire students to dig deep and give themselves fully to their own process.

Compelling storytelling, especially connecting class concepts to personal experiences, is an important skill set for teachers. Moving around the space and using dramatic gestures and strategic pauses, varying expressive vocal range, and changing pace and intonation support engagement. Pausing to ask questions like, "Has anyone ever had that experience?" or "Can you picture that in your mind?" or "What do you think happened next?" can also help hold students' attention.

Of all the strategies mentioned, having well-constructed learning systems that put students in the driver seat is the most important component of engagement. Mastery-based or outcomes-based grading involves starting with valid standards, then drawing those down into a course scope and sequence, instructional units, and daily lesson plans. Each day's learning target (or learning aim, learning purpose, educational target, or similar) is a measurable step on the path of learning the course standards. Assessments match the day's learning target, and allow the teacher to determine if a student has accomplished it. Students are assessed and graded quickly and given specific feedback on this aim, along with support and opportunities to revise if they haven't yet achieved proficiency.

Stepping wholeheartedly into the learning therefore does not imply that a student has to simply comply with a teacher's whims. Feeling bullied into learning is a serious turnoff for many students, especially those who have been abused, mistreated, or neglected in any way. Instead, students are given the goals, support on the path, and the tools they need to unlock key skills for themselves.

It's also important to be intentional about making time purely for the purposes of engagement and community building. We do this by attending carefully to the calendar and planning our scope and sequence so there is space in the year, in given units, and in some cases in given lessons to allow for games, outings, parties, special events, community building, or whatever is needed.

With one class of mostly twelfth graders, the students proposed to reserve Fridays for silent, individual work, and refrain from talking. We set up each week to accommodate this request, using the space in the other classes to revise work, play games, or engage in extra circle discussion time.

This does not mean that if students said, "Come on, Ms. Meghan! Let's forget about the lesson today and practice TikTok dances instead!" I would go along with it. I wouldn't want to give the impression that the lessons are arbitrary or optional. That would likely have the effect of accidentally *decreasing* buy-in—definitely not what I'm going for.

Following the students' lead does not mean we let things get flaky or mushy, or that we let the class meander along solely at the whims of students. We still have to keep the construct clean and stable and attend to rigorous course outcomes. We also have to think about the kids who may have been absent and will not be able to follow the flow if we change it up randomly.

We might say instead, "Well, I worked really hard to set this lesson up for you, and I think you're really going to find it useful. But we can definitely make some time soon to practice dances if everyone in the class wants to." Then, if everyone did vote that they wanted to practice dances, we could have the students who proposed it help to plan the class, and design some time into

Considerations for Engagement

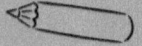

- Classroom or studio is beautiful and inviting
- Instruction is multimodal and varied
- There is a predictable framework and regular protocols
- There are many opportunities for collaboration
- Student leadership and student voice are elevated
- Representation is skillful
- Teachers are receptive to feedback, including challenges
- Successes are highlighted in family communication and classroom
- Teachers are skillful storytellers
- Teachers follow students' lead while retaining rigor
- Teachers have a sense of humor and are honest and humble

the schedule for that activity, or set up a separate time after school or during lunch if the entire class wasn't into it. We have to find a balance that allows space for students' agency and initiative, while avoiding the dangerous trap of random, poorly constructive instruction that lacks urgency or vision.

And please! Please. Above all. Have a sense of humor. Laugh at yourself often. Don't try to hide your fumbles or smooth over your missteps, miscalculations, or failed lessons. Be able to take a joke. When a student is acting like a rascal, raise an eyebrow and survey the room with patient mirth; keep a sense of humor that is tolerant and wise but never makes fun of anyone. Remember that even train wreck moments will pass.

As always, *how* you are is more important than *what* you are, or any one thing you say or do. Avoid toxic positivity, fakeness, or giving too much advice. Kids will sniff you out and will reject your leadership.

Instead be vulnerable and emotionally honest. Even the most challenging of students will benefit from your kindness and authenticity. Very few people can resist a truly open heart for long.

This is love in action.

If you build your classroom around these principles, you will be likely to love your job, your students will be likely to love you, and they may even leave the class loving *themselves* more, which is, after all, really the point of everything.

Chapter Six

Elevating Student Voice and Leadership

> Mindfulness is something that helps us come to touch with ourselves and lay our feet in a real world, not a simulation. It also develops us and helps us see our true selves.
>
> —Zariah Casillas, high school student

As discussed in the chapter on instruction, punishing kids into learning causes more harm than good, and can shore up and deepen the harms of oppression.

Teachers may have to build up an entirely different set of tools for engaging students and getting them to buy in to the work at hand. For some this can be a frightening prospect that will require a total reorientation of what it means to be a teacher.

Make no mistake, this is a paradigm shift. Instead of being an authority and an expert, the teacher instead becomes a facilitator, coach, and cheerleader, who does most of the work *behind* the scenes to set up the conditions for kids to thrive.

Elevating student voice is an area that can be expanded on to help engage students instead of relying on old, punitive strategies.

Any time teachers create opportunities for students to take ownership of their learning and step up as leaders, they are elevating student voice. When teachers step away from center stage, stop norming everything to their own perspective, and invite students to express the truth of their experience, they are also elevating student voice.

When teachers show they care about what students think, value, and believe—and when they demonstrate that all emotions are valid and that students' real experiences matter—they are elevating student voice.

One strategy I use for elevating student voice is very literal. I pull exemplary comments directly from students' written work, then project them the next day. I might ask each student to select which comment stands out the most for them and why. This is a way to deepen and refine their understanding, and also to celebrate and highlight individual students. This strategy also provides urgency, and encourages students to complete work on time.

Another strategy is to gather student representatives into "consultation committees" to help steer and develop course content, classroom protocols, and anything else students believe should be a priority. For a successful consultation committee, it's important to meet regularly, to provide every student the opportunity to have input, and to actually implement some of the students' suggestions. Once a consultation committee starts to have impact, momentum builds quickly.

Additional things teachers can do to elevate student voice include providing low-stakes prompts that every student can weigh in on, quoting students back to themselves in written feedback, creating classroom jobs, sharing quotes or images from student work with families, amplifying the words of students by paraphrasing them, and providing independent opening activities that allow students to teach themselves the content in advance of a mini-lesson.

Using a range of modalities also elevates student voice by providing opportunities for kids to discover and display different talents. Some could include writing, speaking, dance, movement, paraphrasing the teacher or other students, organization, presentations, artwork, design, filmmaking, acting, or facilitation.

Having students lead discussions, meditations, debriefs, and mini-lessons are also excellent ways to elevate student voice.

Another way to elevate student voice is to actively seek opportunities for students to respectfully disagree and push back. Teachers can *say* it's OK to disagree, but it isn't until students actually see it in action and see a teacher respond with receptivity that they start to believe in it as a possibility. Knowing that they can be heard even if they disagree with the teacher teaches kids that their voice matters; and can also be a turning point for trust and buy-in.

There are also things that can be done on the school level to elevate student voice. One is inviting students to lead a meditation or read a poem at a school-wide event or on a loudspeaker, then helping them prepare and supporting them throughout the process. Another is to create a program where older students are paired with a teacher and act as assistant teachers in classrooms with younger students.

When teachers see, honor, and *celebrate* the many gifts that students bring, they are elevating student voice.

If the goal of education is actually to empower the leaders of the future rather than perpetuate the harms of the past, schools need to examine what skills and qualities are being engendered. Teachers will have to give up on the punitive strategies of the previous centuries and instead elevate students' voices in the service of engagement, joy, risk taking, confidence, and leadership.

The future very much depends on it.

Chapter Seven

Working with Resistance

> If you are experiencing emotions, whether that's positive or negative, you must welcome them, show them around in your mind, and embrace them. Whether they're good or bad, they will eventually leave.
>
> —Ibrahim Fudol, high school student

"Let your shoulders relax down. Notice the weight of your body in the chair," I say in a low tone that I hope is soothing. "As the sound fades away, the invitation is to gently turn your attention toward the sensation of breathing."

Jashaun, a student with ADHD, bangs on the door, late to class, and I move to open it, the meditation bell still in hand. He takes his seat with prompting, then closes his eyes and says loudly, "I can feel the humming of the universe pulsing through my body." He is being facetious, and at the same time, he isn't. He's also willing.

I smile and say, "Silently, inside your *own* head, notice when a thought comes. When you do notice a thought, see if you can gently turn your attention back to the breath."

Jashaun continues to vocalize periodically, but seems to move into the energy of the room, taking on the day's mindfulness experiment.

• • •

I've never met a lazy teen. Ever.

I've met teens with serious trust issues as a result of neglect or abuse inside of systems that fail to meet their needs. I've met teens with low self-esteem who are not motivated to do work because they don't believe that anything they do makes a difference. I've also met teens who are shut down because the pain of day-to-day living just feels like too much. And I've met teens who are depressed or so sensitive they can't cope, others who have learning disabilities they haven't learned how to work around, and those who feel guilt, shame, and grief that they have no way to work with.

But I've never met a lazy teen.

One student, a giant football player who towered over his peers, said, "Miss! If I do mindfulness, then I have to deal with *feelings*. I'm not down for all that," while rolling his eyes and leaning backward in his chair.

The biggest reason for resistance is that when we get quiet and start to look inside, feelings we were trying to avoid may rush up to the surface. This can be frightening and painful, especially for those who have experienced trauma such as neglect, abuse, poverty, loss, or repeated experiences of both subtle and overt racism.

Students who have experienced multiple traumas are likely to need extensive modeling, reinforcement, a variety of practice options, and support to even begin to experiment with mindfulness. It is also essential to provide trauma-influenced protocols so students know what to do and how to get support if they are triggered during practice.

Once, when I took a group of students to the schoolyard to do walking meditation, a student who had been previously unreceptive to mindfulness told me the walking meditation helped to clear her head. She then confided that someone in her community had been killed the night before.

When I first started teaching mindfulness in the Brooklyn public high school where I work, I got permission to go into classrooms during my planning period. I knew there was evidence that mindfulness could benefit students, but it remained to be seen if I could find a skillful way to present the work.

During the first weeks, I repeatedly heard, "Why do we have to do this?" "Are we being *graded* for this?" and "Miss! This is too *boring*!"

Learning to work skillfully with resistance is an essential skill set for all teachers, but is particularly important for teachers of mindfulness.

Mindfulness isn't a core requirement, and it may be tempting for students to blow it off. Students may think it's too white, too boring, too annoying, or unlikely to yield benefits for them personally. And what we're asking students to do—to get quiet and look inside themselves—might seem like no big deal, but it can be a seismic shift, even enough to cause internal earthquakes.

In those early days when I was just cutting my teeth as a mindfulness teacher and I was going into other people's classes, some teachers would grade the students for their once-a-week work in our mindfulness sessions. This unsettled me slightly, especially since I hadn't provided the teachers with any specific outcomes or standards, but I did notice that compliance was better in the classes that were being graded, so I pretty much just looked the other way.

By the end of the semester, I noticed something interesting. The classes that were being graded started out better, but the classes where students were *not* being graded ended better. Through dialogue with the kids and careful observation, I came to understand that grading in this way for these once-a-week sessions was working against the goal of authentically engaging the students.

This was food for thought.

I knew that grading for compliance was counterproductive to what I really hoped to achieve. I *could* argue that addressing behavior with punitive grading policies would make it possible for the kids who were already engaged to learn, and that I had to prevent kids who were less compliant from wrecking it for everyone.

But I knew deep down that if I really wanted to provide all students with tools for empowerment, self-awareness, transformation, and self-healing, I was going to have to up my game. I also knew that the least-compliant kids were the ones who could most stand to benefit from mindfulness, and that it was the least-compliant kids I was most passionate about reaching.

The next semester, my principal gave me a daily teaching period to devote to push-in mindfulness instruction. I would use the official mindfulness period and also my teacher preparation and lunch periods to braid my schedule together with teachers' programs so I could push into as many classrooms as possible.

I led with a letter to teachers about what I promised and what I needed if I was going to push into their classes.

In the beginning, not all teachers were willing. They weren't excited to give up instructional time, especially those with high-stakes exams looming in the distance. But as word got around, more and more teachers were willing and even started to seek me out.

In the letter to teachers, I promised to be trustworthy, communicative, and to do my best to benefit students and support their classes. And I asked that they promise to *not* grade the students for mindfulness—at all. I also asked them to trust that I could engage the students authentically, even if it might look messy in the beginning.

There was some grumbling, but there were more takers than I expected. With the exception of just one or two teachers who raised eyebrows and talked trash behind my back, I was surprised to meet very little resistance from adults. In fact, when we opened a mindfulness studio in the school, it was mostly the teachers themselves who contributed to a fundraising campaign to buy meditation cushions for the students.

I was beginning to develop my toolbox in terms of how to work with resistance and engage students authentically.

I provided each student with a brightly colored mindfulness journal, which I produced myself with the school copy machine at the start of each semester. I would have them write down the day's mindfulness technique or skill, note whether they had practiced in the previous week, and respond to a few short writing prompts at the end of each session.

I needed to find ways to make sure that every student could feel seen. Before each class, I responded to what the students had written the previous week and tried to encourage those who had left the page blank. I made sure to respond to every single student's words in some way, even if it was just a smiley face, and I often used these opportunities to support students in developing a nuanced understanding of what the ever-shifting and dynamic quality of mindfulness is.

I learned that one of the best tricks for engagement and working with resistance is to quote the students directly in the next class, and then to use this as a jumping-off point for refining and deepening understanding.

This also created urgency and incentive for students to buy in and do the writing task, and allowed me as a teacher to build relationships with individual students, even if I only interacted with them in a class setting once a week. "That's my conversation with each of you," I would say. And also, "That's how I can tell if I'm doing my job right. Otherwise I really have no way of knowing if I'm being effective or not."

I also learned that if I lead with key lessons, it helps to make resistance less of an issue. It definitely helps to start with brain science and make a compelling, visual, science-based argument for why mindfulness matters in terms of how it impacts the brain.

It's also a good idea to show videos of celebrities with strong student appeal talking about the benefits of mindfulness and meditation.

And all along, providing a lot of personal stories, including why you started meditating and what it has meant for you, and stories by other practitioners (especially practitioners who look like your students) can go a long way toward melting resistance. Inviting previous students to speak to current students about how they have personally benefited from mindfulness is also a great support.

• • •

Many people experience some kind of resistance with mindfulness, especially in the beginning.

When one student brought up that he felt sleepy during the meditation, I offered that sleepiness can be because we didn't get enough sleep and are tired, or sometimes it can come up as a form of resistance. I added, "In some ways our brain wants to keep us from being mindful."

"Why is that?" he asked.

I responded later that day in writing.

> So, we are wired up to be stressed out all the time. We, as feeling creatures, are programmed to try to avoid suffering at all costs.
>
> Becoming mindful means you decide to accept a certain amount of suffering. Like if you're sad, you just feel it. If you feel shy and uncomfortable, you just feel it. Whatever. You don't keep trying to squirm out of everything.
>
> That actually takes a ton of courage. Even though the truth is you're feeling all of that anyway! And once you decide it's OK to feel it, after an initial period when it might feel scary and hard, things usually feel a lot better and more manageable.
>
> So our brain, our ego really (which isn't exactly our brain, but more our mind and our sense of ourself) freaks out when we start to get more mindful because deep down, unconscious, it's so afraid we're gonna feel pain.
>
> The brain sometimes starts to throw up smoke screens, like sleepiness, irritability, super-fast thinking, restlessness, all kinds of stuff . . . to try to get out of the mindfulness at hand.
>
> This is also why we take it really really slow and gentle, so the ego has time to adjust to this new way of being and doesn't freak out as much.

We all have the capacity to be mindful, though those of us who have had traumatic experiences may need extra time and support. In the case of trauma, resistance may be an intelligent, adaptive response to extreme stress, and students might need time to consider new options in light of new circumstances. Trauma-sensitive practice is more thoroughly discussed in the chapter "Trauma-Sensitive Practice and Why Embodiment Matters."

Sometimes there might be receptivity to mindfulness for a period, then a backlash.

At these times we need to communicate that all feelings are normal and acceptable, that feelings are temporary, and that we are there in support, no matter what.

It may be very difficult at first, but each of our students needs to know we are confident they have the power to work with their own experiences when they are ready.

Above all, the key to working with resistance is trust.

Teachers must become totally trustworthy in the minds and nervous systems of their students. There is no way to demand, bribe, or cajole trust. It's real or it isn't. Teens have a keen, precisely attuned bullshit meter. The more teachers try to force students to trust them, the more likely it is that they will instead resent and mistrust their teachers, and deep learning will remain unavailable.

The best advice is receptivity. Validate. Invite.

Never see a student's noncompliance as a threat to your competence or self-image.

It's important to remember that what happens in one class isn't the whole story. Even if one class is a train wreck, the entire arc of the semester or year might have a very different tone.

Often what we see as a personal challenge is actually a student's internal struggle. High school student Celena Kissoon wrote, "Adults think you're being lazy, but really you're fighting your internal demons."[1]

If we react with anger or try to use our authority as teachers to achieve compliance, we are using slash-and-burn teaching, wrecking everything that's alive just to accomplish what we see as our big-picture goal, not considering the long-term impacts of our actions, and perhaps inappropriately trying to reassure our fragile egos and assert our sense of who we think we are.

Through our own practice, we must identify and eliminate the ego stories that make us feel threatened when students resist.

Teaching teens is different from teaching adults. Developmentally, teens are not yet fully able to emotionally self-regulate. They need to be around self-regulated adults who have settled nervous systems, and who they know will have predictable, fair responses. This allows them to feel safe and helps them learn to regulate their own systems.[2]

It doesn't mean we swallow our real feelings in favor of some kind of sanctimonious even temper, but it does mean that we know when we're regulated and when we aren't, and that we know how to take care of our own needs so we can be there for our students.

In a way, this allows us to become their ground.

A slash-and-burn approach (I'm not proud of it, but I have definitely resorted to slash-and-burn teaching at times, especially when I've been co-teaching in poorly managed classrooms) causes more harm than benefit. It is especially problematic for white teachers of students of color to wield authority in this way. Slash-and-burn teaching can be read as oppression. It can deepen the generational traumas of racism and shut students down emotionally as a way to cope with the perceived threat their teachers are presenting. And it most definitely does not support the goal of being trustworthy.

Trying to get students to learn by nagging them incessantly is probably a lesser evil, but is still likely to trigger resistance and may accidentally reinforce a student's self-image of being a reluctant or inadequate learner.

If a student says mindfulness is stupid, we could say something like, "OK, I hear you. Do you want to say anything more about that?" and let them speak. Don't try to argue back or hijack what they are saying. Maybe say something like, "I hear you, and I support you in expressing your opinion. For me, mindfulness has helped a lot, but the only way you will know if it can help you is if you test it out for yourself. Please consider trying out some of the experiments, and continue to ask these kinds of questions. Your experience is important, and I'm glad you shared what you think." Don't try to convince them in the moment. You will be wasting your breath, and it will be counterproductive. Over time, it's likely that the work will speak for itself. There is no need to insist or to oversell it.

Having frequent checks for understanding and gathering feedback constantly can help us monitor how students are receiving the teachings, and can help us stay connected to their unique needs.

When we make a mistake, we need to own it, apologize, and do what we can to fix it. If we invite students to share when we have said or done something that made them upset, and even look for opportunities to invite this kind of feedback publicly, students will be less likely to resist the learning process. There is nothing that builds trust more than students seeing a teacher's humility and receptiveness to hearing a student's true feelings.

If we think there is a chance we might have offended or ignored or failed to see a student, it's a good idea to seek them out as soon as possible and check in with them, and invite them to share their thoughts, even if it seems uncomfortable.

We might think it makes us seem less competent, but the opposite is true. We are simply walking our walk, being willing to truly see and hear, and sit with discomfort without immediately resorting to our patterns for escaping discomfort and pain—exactly what we are trying to teach our students to do.

Making sure to keep families in the loop in terms of what the students are learning, inviting family feedback, and getting to know families are also powerful supports that decrease resistance and help students feel seen and supported.

When a previously resistant student does extend themselves to risk even a tiny bit, I go all out to reinforce it, with praise and by reaching out to families with positive messages.

Another thing is to always invite, not demand. Let students know from the very beginning that they are the boss of their own mind and body, and only they know what is best. I often say, "You are the boss of you. NO ONE knows your needs better than you do." Let them know periodically that if they don't want to try the day's mindfulness experiment, they should do what feels right for them—while, of course, at once setting it up so the obvious thing to do is go with the flow and test it out.

In the NYC teacher rating system, students having their heads down can lead to a lower rating for teachers and is seen as a sign that the teacher doesn't care if a student is disengaged. It took a lot to get people to be OK with allowing students to put their heads down or even put their hoods up during meditations if that felt right, safe, or comfortable. (I would not propose this as an option publicly, but I let it slide for the moment if repeated prompts to "put your body in a position that feels both alert and relaxed" don't get a student to raise their head. Then, I find a different time to privately dialogue with the student about what's going on and how I can support them.)

It's also important for teachers to celebrate and validate students' healthy skepticism, including and especially when racism is implied or overtly mentioned as a factor. This could be especially important for white teachers of students of color. Through pushing back on their teachers, students are learning to advocate for themselves. They are learning that their experiences and

Considerations for Working with Resistance

- Instructions are invitations, not commands
- Activities are presented as experiments
- Student agency is respected
- Teachers don't take student resistance personally
- The possibility that resistance can be a trauma response is considered
- Teachers are trustworthy and honest
- Teachers use a range of strategies to make sure every student feels seen and included
- There are frequent opportunities for feedback and checks for understanding
- Teachers celebrate and validate skepticism
- Former students share their stories with younger students
- Instruction is presented in bite sized pieces and penduluming is used, especially in the beginning

opinions are important. And the more we support students' agency, the more likely they are to authentically buy in to what we are trying to offer.

When I started teaching semester-long and yearlong classes and not just once-a-week push-in sessions, I had to do a lot of tinkering to find systems that would work well for my students.

Of course, we need to have meaningful offerings in terms of course content and tasks. We need to have clean systems tied to specific outcomes. We need to grade things on a regular schedule, to have a solid system for grading, and to be transparent about the goals, methods, and measurements of the class.

I have never graded the actual mindfulness, instead grading students for tasks aligned to the course standards and for their ability to reflect on their experiences.

The things we *don't* want to do: try to punish kids into compliance, nag kids into compliance, reach out to parents in the hopes that they will punish or nag their kids into compliance for us, diminish the validity of kids' resistance, try to force kids to trust us, hold a messy container then use dominance to try to make up for it, and, above all else, we must never allow ourselves to tie our competence or self-worth to anything a student does or lash out in an attempt to squash something that challenges us.

And so we validate, provide support, normalize all feelings that come up, and reassure students that we know they can handle all of their feelings when they are ready, but that if it isn't the right time, that's perfectly OK. They are the only ones who know what is right for them.

Seen in this light, resistance can be viewed as an intelligent response, designed for emotional safety. And it is only with time, trust, and in tiny increments that some students might start to see the benefit of letting go of some of their resistance to try out a new way of being, one that is less constrained by fear and more open to the dance of living, one that can lead down a path to real freedom and to achieving their fullest potential.

NOTES

1. Celena Kissoon, student comment in written classwork, 2021.
2. Desiree W. Murray and Katie Rosanbalm, *Promoting Self-Regulation in Adolescents and Young Adults: A Practice Brief. OPRE Report 2015-82*, Office of Planning, Research and Evaluation, January 31, 2017, https://eric.ed.gov/?id=ED594226

Chapter Eight

Mindfulness Instruction

Practicing is about discipline and habit, not about if you feel like it. I can use that in my practice too, by still practicing even though I don't want to sometimes.

—Elia Riebl, high school student

In a deep state of meditation, you can find your true self. Only you know your true self, nobody can tell you who you "are" because only you know.

—Obdulia Zuluaga, high school student

"Sit up like the royalty you are, with a feeling of dignity and power, and at the same time, relaxed, and feeling your connection to the ground." My voice is even and low, leading an opening meditation. "See if there's any part of your body that could be five to ten percent more soft, more relaxed. And take a breath in. And attention to sound." At this point, I ring a three-tone chime. As the sound fades away, I invite students to switch their attention to the feeling of the body breathing.

Sometimes I provide images or models. On this day, we settle deeply into the rhythm of the breath. After we follow the breath for two or three minutes, today I say, "If it feels OK for you, with your eyes closed, see if you can sense the inside of you. Maybe like the inside of your belly, your lungs, your throat." After a pause, I say, "It's inside here, where your power is. That's what you're tapping into now. Your power is inside you. It doesn't come from any outside person, any outside place," I intone. "That power is there simply because you were born, a shining human being. It is your birthright. More and more, you are learning how to connect with that place of power that is always there inside you."

Some boil down mindfulness for students to "just be in the moment." But the fact is that teens need extensive modeling, support, a range of practice options, opportunities to discuss and integrate experiments, and opportunities to ask questions, push back, and test things out for themselves.

Mindfulness is a challenging subject to convey, and it requires us to show up with top-notch instruction, expert student engagement skills, and our own embodied example of practice. We also need to hold space skillfully and have a wide, nonreactive bandwidth for all that students bring.

As discussed in the chapter "Working with Resistance," it's important to move very gently into meditation practices, and to present them in bite-size pieces, especially in the beginning.

Mindfulness classes for teens will necessarily be mostly concerned with social and emotional learning topics that mindfulness opens up, such as Pausing, Responsible Decision Making, Communication Skills, Healthy Relationships, Dealing with Difficult Emotions, Growth Mindset, Empathy, and Social Justice. I base grades entirely on how students relate to these topics, and on students' ability to reflect on their own practice, but never on the actual mindfulness.

This chapter will focus on teaching the actual mindfulness practices.

"What's the big deal? You just ring a bell and close your eyes," one student tells me, explaining how anyone can do my job.

I have to smile. Of course, I don't get into it with her, but there actually *is* more to it—mostly because there are so many ways you can go wrong.

Every teacher would do well to include social and emotional learning as part of every unit and every lesson, and to make time for mindfulness by adding planned pauses, asking reflective questions, and helping students to identify and describe how they are feeling; but if you want to actually teach mindfulness practice, it's important to have had significant practice experience.

You are the teaching. They have to want what you got. Period. There are no words that can replace what you, in your person, bring. You will have to be very present, clear, and practiced to pull this off. You will have to have had plenty of firsthand experience of where practice can go off the rails so you can help usher students along their own paths. There's no need to present yourself as an expert. Let your vibe speak for itself.

First and foremost, in the words of 5Rhythms teacher and NYC assistant principal Kierra Foster-Ba, "We invite, we don't command." Forcing students to meditate will backfire.

I had one co-teacher in an academic classroom who decided we should get students to meditate at the beginning of class each day. This was a poorly managed classroom, so that in effect looked like setting a timer and telling kids they had to be quiet for several minutes. He would scowl and gesture angrily if anyone whispered, and outright scream if anyone spoke aloud. In this case, it did more harm than good; and it was like trying to keep a lid on a volcano.

Students need to enter into mindfulness on their own terms and in their own time. If we present it not as a mandate but as an experiment—conveying that it will probably help them, but they will only know if they test it out for themselves—students are more likely to be receptive. That said, it's important to be careful not to accidentally emphasize that there are too many outs. Ideally, we make testing out the mindfulness experiments we propose seem like the obvious and most appealing choice, but we don't force it if and when kids push back.

Before any attempt at practice, I start with a compelling lesson on the brain science of mindfulness, and provide videos and images of people who look like my students discussing the benefits of meditation.

I also tell my own story of how I came to mindfulness and how it has impacted me.

Instruction builds in tiny increments, a little bit each day.

The first thing is the body. I say something like, "For this, we're going to experiment with what it would be like to have our bodies in a mindful posture—that's a shape that feels both dignified and powerful, and also at the same time relaxed. Once I ring this bell, I invite you to test out a mindful posture." Usually very little has happened, but I say, "OK that looks good, everyone. Now let's go back into *whatever*-body posture." Then I demonstrate with my own bizarre "whatever posture," flopping myself dramatically. I try to make this playful. I say, "OK, when I ring the bell again, I want to see you go back into a mindful posture, then we'll go back to whatever posture. I really want to see the difference between the two. Ready?" We might even toggle between whatever posture and mindful posture a few times. I then invite students to share if they feel any different in "whatever-posture" compared to "mindful-posture," and repeat the experiment.

Usually by this point most of the group is buying in, though there are likely to be a few holdouts. The language could be adapted, but starting with the body is an essential building block, and finding the tone that is least likely to trigger resistance is important.

We start pretty much every meditation with anchoring ourselves in the body.

The second anchor we work with is sound. I say, "OK, everyone. In a minute I'm going to ring this bell. Our experiment for today is to try to see if you can keep your mind on the bell sound for the entire time. See if you can notice the *exact millisecond* that the sound totally disappears. Then, you just raise your hand," I say while raising my hand to demonstrate. After we go through that first process, I ask if anyone felt like they were able to keep their mind on the bell sound for the entire time. I ask if anyone felt like it was hard to keep their mind on the sound. We go through the process again, and sometimes even a third time.

The three classic anchors are body, sound, and breath, but we can really use anything as an anchor. In mindfulness traditions, the anchor is sometimes called a "primary object." It just means the main thing you're keeping your attention on. When you notice your attention drifts, you gently bring it back to the anchor. Not only does this build up focus and improve our ability to be with the present moment, we also start to notice whatever our brain is doing when it is *not* on the anchor before we shepherd it back. This can lead to many important insights.

The next step—sometimes this is in the same session, sometimes this is a building block that gets added on in a later session—is to say, "OK, once the bell sound totally fades away, and we raise our hands, we're going to lower them again, and then we're going to open up our attention to all the sounds we can hear." Then I guide them through the first bell process, adding on the new step. Afterward, I go around and ask each student to share what sounds they noticed.

I might debrief with questions like, "What was it like for you to pay attention to sounds like this? What was it like when you were trying to keep attention on the sound? Did you notice any new sounds that you weren't aware of before?" With questions like this, it's best not to go around and ask everyone to share—this kind of redundancy makes teens roll their eyes—but I would open it up to volunteers. When students do share, I try to respond to their comments in a way that can deepen everyone's understanding, and I'm careful to make sure students don't regret that they spoke in front of the class. As usual, I might propose a second round once students have had a chance to share.

I validate any feelings that come up, including peacefulness, irritation, or any other, but at this point, my prompts don't include anything about feelings. For students who have trauma or are sensitive, that can produce a red alert. At this point, I'm trying to help them get some experience with the felt sense of mindfulness in a tiny dose, then leading them out of it fairly quickly. It's also important to give everyone the opportunity to integrate it through discussion and reflection before pressing forward. Following the debrief, I might lead a second round of the same experiment, since there is likely to be more engagement after some students share what the experiment was like for them.

The next step might be in the same session or the following, very much depending on receptivity and whether or not anyone in the group is starting to be triggered. At this point I add the instruction to see if you can keep your attention on sound, and when your mind shifts away and starts doing something else, see if you can gently bring the attention back to sound. As usual, we debrief after.

After the first building block, I again start with the body, then move to the bell sound, then from there to opening attention to all sounds. All of this is guided with a patient, calm voice. I might add prompts and reminders about relaxing different body parts, and about attention.

In responding to what students share, I paraphrase and acknowledge students' feelings. Sometimes I want to riff off of what they say, too. In this case I start with, "I know this isn't what you said, but it's making me think of something I'd like to add on," so they don't feel like I hijacked what they were saying for my own purposes.

Most importantly, I make sure to normalize whatever feelings come up, saying in practically every single session, "All sorts of different feelings might come up. That's totally normal. We might feel energetic, annoyed, sad, bored, peaceful, sleepy. Any type of way." We can take this in many different directions, but the core message is the same, when it comes to feelings, there is no "should." We all have the capacity to experience every single emotion, and however we feel is completely fine, normal, and acceptable.

And we, ourselves, really have to believe this. We, ourselves, have to hold space with such clarity and nonjudgment that students feel safe to relax into the full force of feeling, which can be extremely painful and challenging. Once we get quiet and briefly pause the unending flow of busyness and entertainment, suppressed feelings may quickly rise to the surface.

Teens care a lot about how they're seen, so being honest about feelings is extra loaded. If they have also been impacted by trauma or even multiple traumas, they may believe that their feelings are too volatile and overwhelming to let out of their box.

For some students, just being able to settle the body down can take a long time. If a student has learned hypervigilance as a coping mechanism, it might be frightening to let the body soften and relax out of fight-flight. Deep breathing, counting breaths, and attention to body sensations or the feet on the floor can help encourage this step in the process.

Penduluming, the term used by trauma specialist Bessel van der Kolk and others, means to dip very slightly into the places that are most loaded, then swing back out.[1] We can use a similar practice in guiding students in initial mindfulness experiments. In addition, some students might require support from counselors or other trained adults.

Once we start to be able to settle the body, we can start to develop the ability to concentrate on our chosen object, and from there it's much easier to track the movements of our attention. This is the territory of mindfulness.

Another reason it's so important for us to hold a safe, nonjudgmental container is from a developmental perspective. According to brain scientists, humans don't fully develop the ability to emotionally self-regulate until we are in our mid-twenties.[2] Because of this, it is quite literally the regulated nervous systems of the adult leaders in the room that provide the ground for students to open up to their own experiences.

That's why we ourselves need to have significant, embodied practice experience. Otherwise, we will not be able to move students beyond calming down and basic self-care.

As mindfulness teachers, it's also important to find the right emphasis for our students, as mindfulness touches into such a big range of themes.

Near the beginning of the movement for racial reckoning following the murder of George Floyd, empathy was a theme in one of my daily talks. Something wasn't sitting right with me, but I couldn't name it right away. Later that day, I realized that teaching about empathy to teens of color in that particular moment was completely the wrong emphasis. It's not that my students couldn't connect with empathy, they certainly could, but more that I was setting up the wrong frame, lacking sensitivity to what my students needed, and failing to realize that I might be making an inappropriate request. I failed to place the right emphasis.

There are many things we might choose to emphasize in mindfulness instruction, but I tend to foreground empowerment, especially for teens who may be under-resourced and burdened with trauma.

Although mindfulness makes us calmer, it's not really about calming down. It's not about compliance in classrooms. It's not crowd control. If anything, it's there to shake us up, to connect us with our vast, inner power, and to lay bare the false narratives that society imposes upon us.

Mindfulness is about seeing the truth. As we learn to place our mind on a chosen object, such as sounds or the breath, our mind gradually begins to settle down. A traditional metaphor is a glass of muddy water that grows clear as it grows still, the mud eventually settling to the bottom. Thus, as we are more able to see what's happening in the mind, we are more able to identify our thoughts as they come and to see them for what they are, which is often garbage we've internalized from our society, including racist narratives that make us forget who we are—shining, infinitely powerful, innately perfect, and unfathomably interconnected.

Some mindfulness teachers love to emphasize compassion. That's nice and all, but this can also be a very edgy, warrior-ish, courageous thing we're doing here.

If we emphasize compassion too much, it winds up overshadowing the sticky, complicated mess that is the reality of being alive, and we stay right on the surface, missing opportunities for lasting transformation and healing.

After the first process of coming into awareness of the body and the second process of coming into awareness of sound, the third doorway is breath.

Breath-centered meditation is the core practice of mindfulness meditation. It's mostly because the breath is always with us. It also reminds us we are alive; it is constantly moving and changing; it connects our external and internal experience; and it can key us in to our emotional shifts.

After we experiment with resting attention on sound, we dive into the breath. First, I invite students to take several big breaths in. Then I ask them to pay careful attention and see if they can notice where they feel the breath most strongly. In this case, I go around the room and invite each person to share. Most pick the chest or belly, but it could also be the nose, ribcage, back, or any other body part.

I tell them we call this the "Anchor Breath." I also show them an image of a ship with an anchor, and we talk about what a ship's anchor does, and how that relates to this idea of Anchor Breath. I say, "This is your personal Anchor Place; that means whenever you want to switch into mindfulness of breath, you know exactly where to bring your attention. You don't even have to stop and think about it." We go through our process again, settling and coming into awareness of the body, then ringing a bell and paying attention to its sound, then shifting attention to the breath. All of this is carefully guided, and there are many opportunities to share, question, and integrate.

Again, this is slow and served up in bite-size pieces. With rare exceptions, the actual mindfulness instruction is mostly embedded inside lessons and units on topics that are related to mindfulness rather than as stand-alone lessons.

Finding ways to give mindfulness practice itself density so it feels intentional and not random is important in helping students to develop their practice. Because mindfulness practice is so *not* concrete, this has to be carefully constructed.

One way to help give practice density is to hold one-to-one conferences with students to ask how practice is going for them, especially after the first week or two. The way I accomplish this is to plan for days in the calendar when students will be working independently, and invite them to sit with me one at a time, then ask what they are noticing, and listen actively and intently. At this point, some will have a lot to say, some will shrug and not say much. That's completely fine. The fact that I'm asking shows that I care, that this process is something I'm committed to sharing with them, and that their internal experience matters.

Another way is to have very specific questions during practice debriefs. For example, if I'm teaching a practice that involves counting breaths, I might go around and invite each student to share how many breaths they got up to before their mind started to wander, and what they did when they noticed their mind had wandered.

It's important to build up a cache of supporting metaphors and images that work well for your students.

One metaphor students tend to like is comparing directing the mind to house training a puppy. This is how I spin it, "When we're training a puppy to go to the bathroom on a mat instead of all over the house, we put down the mat, and we show the puppy where she's supposed to go. Then, when she goes somewhere else instead, we gently pick her up and bring her to the mat, saying, 'Here, puppy, this is where you need to go.' When the same thing happens again, we pick her up and bring her to the mat again. It's not like we scream at the cute little puppy and get all upset just because she hasn't learned where to go yet. We just pick her up, show her what we want her to do again and again. And eventually she gets the idea and starts going on the mat instead of all over the apartment. In the same way, we patiently keep bringing the mind back to the breath. Eventually it becomes a stronger habit, and it's easier for us to keep our attention on the one thing we chose."

At times, we can emphasize that mindfulness is learning to stay in the present, even when it is uncomfortable. Teaching a practice that invites students to notice when their thoughts drift to the past or the future is a great way to deepen practice, and also helps them begin to notice the habits of mind that repeatedly take us away from the present. When we notice that students are starting to have insights into these kinds of habits of mind, it's important to give them many opportunities to reflect in writing and to discuss with peers.

I keep a poster in the mindfulness studio that we add to every time we experiment with a new practice. Though breath-centered meditation is the baseline, we also experiment with loving-kindness practice, self-compassion practice, walking meditation, mindful eating, three-part breathing, and speaking and listening practice, among others. (See appendix for descriptions of student friendly mindfulness practices.)

New practices are ideally tied to the social and emotional topics and units we are working on and are layered in slowly, with plenty of time for discussion and integration.

To support students in developing their personal practice, I miss no chance to promote the following essential attitudes that support mindfulness, which are adapted from *Mindfulness in Plain English* by Bhante Gunaratana.[3]

1. Don't expect anything: Just sit back and see what happens. Treat the whole thing as an experiment. Take an active interest in the test itself. But don't get distracted by your expectations about results. For that matter, don't be anxious for any result whatsoever. Let the meditation teach you what it wants you to learn.
2. Don't strain: Don't force anything or be extra. Meditation is not aggressive. Just let your effort be relaxed and steady. Remember, consistency yields results!
3. Don't rush: There is no hurry, so take you time. Settle yourself on a cushion and imagine you have the whole day. Anything really valuable takes time to develop. Patience, patience, patience.
4. Don't cling onto anything and don't push anything away: Let whatever comes step inside the door, whatever it is. If good stuff comes up, that is fine. If bad stuff comes up, that is fine, too. Try to make yourself comfortable with whatever happens. Don't fight with what you experience, just observe it all mindfully. (Except if you are getting trauma-triggered and you need to use the What to Do if You Are Trauma-Triggered steps.)
5. Let go: Learn to flow with all the changes that come up. Loosen up and relax.
6. Accept everything that arises: Accept your feelings, even the ones you wish you didn't have. Accept your experiences, even the ones you hate. Don't be hard on yourself for having normal human flaws. Learn to see all that happens in the mind as being perfectly natural and understandable. (Except if you are getting trauma-triggered and you need to use the What to Do if You Are Trauma-Triggered steps.)
7. Be gentle with yourself: You may not be perfect, but you are all you've got to work with. The process of becoming who you will be begins first with the total acceptance of who you are now.
8. Investigate for yourself: Question everything. Don't believe something just because somebody said it. See for yourself. That does not mean that you should be rude. It means you should test everything with your real experience and let that be your guide to truth. The entire practice of mindfulness depends on us being hungry to find out the truth. Without it, the practice is just superficial (on the surface, not deep).
9. View all problems as challenges: Look upon negatives and challenges as opportunities to learn and to grow. Sometimes this is where we can learn the most. We can have a growth mindset about our practice.
10. Don't overthink: You don't need to figure everything out. The idea is that the mind is purified naturally by mindfulness, you just have to keep doing the practice and trusting the practice. You don't have to figure everything out first in order to heal yourself.

11. Be curious: Whatever comes up in your experience, however blissful or agonizing, can be the object of your fascination. It might even be the key to unlocking new insights and capacities. Being curious allows us to relate to our experiences as precious teachings, even if they challenge us.

Once students have established a basic practice, I like to introduce the idea that meditation engages both concentration and mindfulness. In the beginning, it will all sound like synonyms to them but, once there is a foundation, this concept can help to refine practice and bring about increased engagement and deepening of practice. Most people tend to be naturally stronger in either concentration or mindfulness.

Concentration is focus. It's the ability to direct the mind to a certain object or task. When we practice bringing the mind back to the chosen object, such as the breath, we are increasing our concentration.

Mindfulness, on the other hand, is more related to awareness. It is the flexible monitoring of all that arises in the flow of consciousness with an open and curious attitude, even as things are constantly shifting and changing. Some level of concentration is needed in order to develop mindfulness.

Attributes of Skillful Mindfulness Instruction

- Mindfulness and meditation are extensively modeled
- Diverse representations of mindfulness practitioners and experts are presented, and reflect students' own identities
- A compelling, science-based argument is made early on
- Mindfulness is embedded into related units or topics
- Students have many opportunities to discuss and reflect
- Mindfulness is presented in bite-sized pieces
- Student agency is respected and empowerment is emphasized
- Teachers work to give practice "density" by including some concrete practices, conferencing frequently, and taking student comments seriously
- Penduluming makes mindfulness more approachable including for students with trauma

Settling the body—the critical process of allowing ourselves to relax out of fight-flight, hypervigilance, and sympathetic activation—is related to both of these qualities. Settling the body supports concentration and mindfulness; and concentration and mindfulness support us in settling the body.

All instruction is supported by elevating student voice and utilizing students as leaders, and mindfulness is no exception. To highlight student voice, I quote the students from their own classwork and use this as the starting point for the following day's teachings. I also include low-stakes, compelling prompts that allow every student to weigh in on most days. And students themselves learn to guide mindfulness practice and often take the reins, moving to the front of the mindfulness studio and taking over the teacher's chair. Students also take turns facilitating small groups, leading schoolwide mindfulness practices, explaining key topics, hosting guests and visitors to the program, and serving on consultation committees on a range of topics.

To reiterate, mindfulness instruction for teens is supported by: going slowly and delivering instruction in bite-size pieces; respecting students' agency; holding a safe, nonjudgmental container; right emphasis; and the teacher's own embodied example.

It's important to be inclusive in terms of what we consider to be mindfulness, especially since there can be a branding problem that connects mindfulness with white people. Many things can cultivate mindfulness—dancing, playing music, drawing, and playing basketball are a few examples. Even with that said, explicitly developing the specific quality of mindfulness is worth the effort, as it unlocks self-awareness and a whole range of possibilities that support us in every other area.

Powerful, explicit mindfulness instruction is like handing a kid a sharp sword and arming them with the tools they need to cut through obstacles and thrive; and we owe it to our children to provide them with every possible tool at our disposal.

NOTES

1. Bessel van der Kolk, *The Body Keeps the Score: Mind, Brain and Body in the Transformation of Trauma* (London: Penguin, 2015).
2. Desiree W. Murray and Katie Rosanbalm, *Promoting Self-Regulation in Adolescents and Young Adults: A Practice Brief. OPRE Report 2015-82*, Office of Planning, Research and Evaluation, January 31, 2017, https://eric.ed.gov/?id=ED594226
3. Bhante Gunaratana, *Mindfulness in Plain English* (Somerville: Wisdom, 2019).

Chapter Nine

Trauma-Sensitive Practice and Why Embodiment Matters

> The body, not the thinking brain, is where we experience most of our pain, pleasure, and joy, and where we process most of what happens to us. It is also where we do most of our healing, including our emotional and psychological healing.
>
> —Resmaa Menakem, *My Grandmother's Hands: Racialized Trauma and the Pathway to Mending Our Hearts and Bodies*

> People become so imprisoned by their minds that they go crazy on the inside, and they forget what got them there and why they're still there at that moment.
>
> —Zariah Casillas, high school student

"Can we come in, please? This is one of my favorite students; and she's really suffering today." Turning to the student I've just accompanied to the counselor's office, I ask, "Is it OK if I tell the counselor a little bit about what's coming up before I go back to the classroom?"

A similar scene plays out again and again, especially in the first few weeks of mindfulness class.

According to the American Academy of Pediatrics, more than two thirds of US teens have had at least one adverse childhood experience—a potentially traumatic event such as violence, abuse, losing a parent, or growing up in a family with addiction problems.[1]

As a result of systemic injustice, Black, Indigenous, and other children of color are more likely to have experienced potentially traumatic events, including the impacts of racism itself.[2] Race-based traumatic stress, or racialized trauma, is the cumulative effects of individual and systemic racism on mental and physical health.³ Like other forms of trauma, race-based traumatic stress writes itself into the body.

Trauma specialist, healer, therapist, and author Resmaa Menakem explains the impacts of centuries of racialized trauma. "As many researchers now believe, the ongoing violations of the Black body and heart have resulted in widespread trauma. This racialized trauma shows up as an array of adaptive but dysfunctional behaviors, including hypervigilance, heightened anxiety and suspicion, ADHD, Obsessive-Compulsive Disorder, and addiction."⁴

In a mindfulness classroom, we will inevitably encounter students who are coping with trauma and mental health challenges. Most of us are not trauma experts, but we need to be able to support our students as skillfully as possible. Some students will also need the support of a counselor once they start to tune in to their internal landscape, perhaps contacting feelings they have been suppressing.

It might seem tempting to avoid opening a Pandora's box to the potential minefield of trauma. But just because trauma isn't immediately obvious doesn't mean it isn't having an impact. At the extreme, students might act out as a way to cope with seemingly unbearable feelings. But often, trauma lies just under the surface, casting the pall of anxiety over everything, toning down joy, numbing us, and causing us to reach for escape behaviors. In the words of high school student Cree Washington, "Anxiety makes me shy."⁵ Thus, students are robbed of the opportunity to individuate, to find and commit to their passions, and to become their full selves. The world is also robbed of their brilliance and unique contributions.

Students who suffer from the most trauma might be the most difficult to engage in mindfulness practices, but they might also be the ones who stand the most to benefit.

Although it can be painful and frightening to begin to come into the present and into the body, especially if there is a heavy load of trauma, and it might not be safe or possible right away for a given student, we actually need the trauma, memories, and painful assumptions students are carrying to rise up to consciousness at some point so they can be addressed.

In an ideal world, students with a lot of trauma would have individual and group counseling with qualified therapists they feel identified with. They would have explicit ongoing instruction in social, emotional, and life skills from preschool on. They would have healthy ways to move their bodies. They would have access to the resources they need to get their basic needs met and build their career path. They would also have loving and supportive families, teachers, and communities to help them process their experiences and move into adult life intact and with all the tools they need.

But we don't live in an ideal world. Even in the best possible scenarios, youth mental health problems are skyrocketing. In addition, systemic racism impacts the likelihood that our kids will get all of their needs met. Our kids urgently need healing spaces and processes.

Many see schools as the best place for this work because of their wide reach and important role in the lives of children and families; and a mindfulness classroom has the potential to help create the conditions students need for self-healing.[6]

Trauma causes us to become disembodied.

In order to protect ourselves from further harm, trauma causes us to distance from the body and limit mindfulness. We may become dissociative, numb, or chronically distracted. Instead of attending to the present moment, we learn to constantly scan past experiences for clues about how to avoid future pain; and our brain keeps up a constant rush of analysis. This analysis distances us from our unfolding experiences in this present moment, and makes it hard for us to feel content, connected, or inspired.

Healing from trauma involves recovering our healthy connection to our bodies. Thus, trauma-sensitive practice is embodied practice.

Resmaa Menakem argues that since trauma is a process in the body, the path to healing trauma is also through the body, and may happen independent of cognitive processes.[7]

In addition to trauma, ongoing unexamined societal pressures and developmental processes can lead to disembodiment, anxiety, and the inability to feel at ease.

Because of this, highly effective mindfulness instruction emphasizes, models, and includes embodied practice.

The first layer of embodied practice starts with how the teacher shows up in the room. Developmentally, teens are not yet fully able to regulate their own nervous systems. The teacher's ability to self-regulate their own nervous system can allow students to begin to co-regulate and eventually to self-regulate.[8]

This does not mean that the teacher has to be an imperturbable sage but that they are often grounded, and have the tools to work with their experiences when dysregulated.

This has everything to do with the teacher's commitment to their own self-care and personal mindfulness practices.

Resmaa Menakem also argues that trauma can also be seen as an event that was never completed harmoniously and instead got stuck in the body. In this case, we might help students to symbolically or literally complete the action.[9]

I once met a little girl with a tiny cast on her arm. I watched as she brought a doll to the top of a sloped couch arm, then traveled the doll down again and again while quietly talking it through. Her mother shared that she had broken her arm on the slide at the playground. This was the girl's intuitive way of working the experience through her system, of completing the action so it wouldn't linger in her body as trauma.

We can encourage students to intentionally create a gesture or personal ritual to address trauma they have experienced. Another thing we can do is invite intuitive movement with skillful prompting to give students the opportunity to tune in to their bodies' innate wisdom in finding the movements needed for their own healing process.

It's also important to explicitly teach students about trauma, including the fact that most people in the United States have experienced some trauma in their lives. Students also need to know that trauma isn't just an event that happened but the ongoing response of the body and mind to that event. In some cases, we might have trauma that we don't consciously know about but that is nonetheless impacting us.

• • •

After teaching about trauma, I share the following steps, post them in the classroom, and refer to them often:

WHAT TO DO IF YOU'RE TRIGGERED DURING PRACTICE:

1. *Notice* that you feel something
2. *Pause* and list everything you can notice (heart beating fast, sweating, breathing, etc.)
3. *Decide* if you will still do the experiment the class is doing or if you will do something different
4. *Get support* if needed

The third step, *decide,* is when students make a decision about if they will continue with the practice the group is doing, or if they will change to a different activity. If it's a time when they have the ability to be curious and brave, they can continue with the practice to see what unfolds.

If it's not the right time, and they feel excessively overwhelmed, they can switch practices—perhaps shifting from an internal focus to an external one. They should be provided with options that can ease the triggered response of the sympathetic nervous system until they can begin to settle the body enough to come back to mindfulness. Some examples are looking around the environment to find everything of a certain color, noticing one thing for each of the senses, or orienting toward sound in the environment. They can also switch to gentle stretching or shifting the weight from side to side.

Students who are struggling with a lot of anxiety thinking especially might need calming activities that will actually distract them from their persistent thoughts at times. Some examples are coloring, drawing, reading, listening to music, taking a walk, or talking with a friend. It's important to have options ready to deploy and to be in regular conversation with students about their needs.

Even as we provide alternatives as needed, students need to know we have complete confidence that they will be able to move with their experiences once they are ready, and that we will be there to support them when the time comes.

Moving into mindfulness practice in tiny increments is also essential, as is providing students with plenty of time to discuss and integrate their experiences.

Bessel van der Kolk, the trauma specialist who proposed the neurobiological model for PTSD, advocates "penduluming" in therapeutic work with patients who have experienced trauma. Penduluming means you dip in just a little, then back away. The next time, you might dip in just a little more.[10] With mindfulness instruction for teens, penduluming can also be helpful.

Trauma can also show up as resistance. When students first start to turn inward, they may experience a surge of seemingly overwhelming feelings and sensations, and push back as a way to protect themselves.

Letting students know that they are in charge of their own process, and that only *they* know what they most need is essential. Interpreting resistance as a learned, adaptive response to pain, rather than as an affront to teacher authority, supports us in moving with sensitivity.

The phrase "You've got to feel it to heal it" hits home for many students, and can offer hope that there is a purpose for working through the difficult parts of their experience.

Another way to encourage students is to share the idea that if we can stay even briefly present with difficult feelings and emotions when they come up, they get filed back into the brain in a different place. This can mean they are less likely to control us all the time.

Although counseling can be very helpful, students don't always have to mentally understand their experiences to heal from them. Sometimes simply paying attention to a wave of emotion as it moves through, taking a body shape, or moving intuitively may resolve emotions that have become stuck and heal us even more than talking about it. According to the creator of the 5Rhythms dance and movement meditation practice, Gabrielle Roth, if you "put your body in motion . . . your psyche will heal itself."[11]

To help students be more present in their bodies, teachers can encourage patient attention to the body during sitting, walking, or movement meditation, including prompts and discussion that draw attention to bodily sensations. We can also encourage students to notice which parts of the body feel relaxed and which feel tense or tight, and to pay attention as these states shift. This supports the process of self-healing and helps students reestablish the ability to tolerate the present moment.

Additional classroom practices that support embodiment include narrating our own physical sensations and underscoring when a student shares about sensation in the body, designing games and collaborative activities that encourage movement, creating colorful drawing interpretations of the emotional body, and using body scan practices wherein students are guided to notice sensations throughout the body.

Yoga, stretching, conscious dance practices, acting, and tai chi can also support embodiment and self-healing.

It's important to keep in mind that students might not be ready or may not have the right conditions at a given moment to move into trauma head on. That could be for a variety of reasons, including the possibility that students of color might not feel an embodied sense of safety with a white teacher. In this case, we can let students know that we have complete confidence that a time will come when they are ready, and that we know they will be able to move into and through the difficult places to heal themselves when the time is right.

Trauma writes itself into our brains and bodies, our identities and our imaginations. It can bar us from realizing our full potential and living with ease and joy.

Steps for Students to Follow if Triggered During Practice:

1. **Notice** that you feel something
2. **Pause** and list everything you can notice (heart beating fast, sweating, breathing, etc)
3. **Decide** if you will still do the experiment the class is doing or if you will do something different
4. **Get Support** if needed

The very real chance of re-traumatizing vulnerable students must guide us, but shying away from any possibility of triggering trauma closes down the opportunity for healing and transformation that so many of our precious youth must have in order to step into their full power and potential.

NOTES

1. Marci Hertz et al., "Adverse Childhood Experiences among US Adolescents over the Course of the COVID-19 Pandemic," *Pediatrics* 151, no. 6 (June 2023): 1–9, https://doi.org/10.1542/peds.2022-060799

2. Xiaoyan Zhang and Shannon M. Monnat, "Racial/Ethnic Differences in Clusters of Adverse Childhood Experiences and Associations with Adolescent Mental Health." *SSM—Population Health* 17, no. 100997 (December 2021): 1–9, https://doi.org/10.1016/j.ssmph.2021.100997

3. "Racial Trauma," Mental Health America, accessed August 8, 2023, https://www.mhanational.org/racial-trauma

4. Resmaa Menakem, *My Grandmother's Hands: Racialized Trauma and the Pathway to Mending Our Hearts and Bodies* (London: Penguin, 2021).

5. Cree Washington, student comment in written classwork, 2020.

6. Stephanie Wilde et al., "Mindfulness Training in UK Secondary Schools: A Multiple Case Study Approach to Identification of Cornerstones of Implementation," *Mindfulness* 10, no. 4 (June 4, 2019), https://www.ncbi.nlm.nih.gov/pmc/articles/PMC6558285/

7. Menakem, *My Grandmother's Hands*.

8. Desiree W. Murray and Katie Rosanbalm, *Promoting Self-Regulation in Adolescents and Young Adults: A Practice Brief. OPRE Report 2015-82*. Office of Planning, Research and Evaluation, January 31, 2017, https://eric.ed.gov/?id=ED594226

9. Menakem, *My Grandmother's Hands*.

10. Bessel van der Kolk, *The Body Keeps the Score: Mind, Brain and Body in the Transformation of Trauma* (London: Penguin, 2015).

11. Gabrielle Roth and John Loudon, *Maps to Ecstasy: Teachings of an Urban Shaman* (London: Thorsons, 1995).

Chapter Ten

Dealing with Difficult Emotions and Discomfort

> My days were filled with tragedy
> Days when I felt like committing
> Assault and battery.
> Some days I felt like an untamed
> Beast.
> Through the power of mindfulness
> I was able to express my feelings
> And let them go.
> I wish I would have known
> That I could live in peace.
> Life used to be hard for
> Me.
> I constantly lost people,
> I felt miserable and depressed.
> Now I can finally breathe
> And get pain off my chest.
>
> —Gianni Douglas, high school student

I deal with a bad day by pausing and reminding myself that bad days happen to everyone and that they pass.

—Cailyn Miller, high school student

When we have a lot of uncertainty we tend to have a stress response. Our bodies start shutting down so instead of shutting down, relax into it and see what happens as it's happening to your body. The more we close down it's more tiring, making us feel less alive. To some extent relaxing acts as a reliever.

—Anonymous, high school student

There are many available modalities for students to process feelings, reflect on experiences, and learn life skills, but mindfulness is unique in that all emotions are met with an attitude of curiosity and receptivity—even painful and difficult emotions like fear, sadness, anxiety, and anger.

In order to address difficult emotions with adolescents, a lot of groundwork has to be laid down in advance. First and foremost, students need to feel safe and included in the classroom. There need to be clear, predictable systems and protocols for daily lessons, grading, assessment, and feedback. Students also need to have a foundation in basic mindfulness practice, including an embodied understanding of what mindfulness feels like in the body. On top of all that, students need to deep-down, full-on trust the adult in the room.

Developmentally, adolescents are not yet fully capable of regulating their own nervous systems—being able to move between different states of energy in response to stressors and their environments. The prefrontal cortex especially, which regulates thoughts, actions, and emotions, is nowhere near mature in teens. To help them learn to regulate their own systems, they need practiced, stable adults who can hold space, model what it means to be regulated, and help them learn to regulate themselves.[1]

And they need to be regulated in order to have the capacity for risk that will allow them to step into the deeper waters of their internal experiences.

It takes time and patience to develop this foundation. Rushing or pushing students to start dealing with difficult emotions right away might actually cause more harm than good. Instead, allowing them to interact with less-loaded topics such as healthy habits, mindful communication, and growth mindset is recommended to help set the stage.

Early in the year, long before any discussion of difficult emotions, I offer students a unit called "The Power of Pausing," inviting them to start experimenting with pausing as a strategy for emotional regulation as a first step toward dealing with difficult emotions. Much later, once we are further along our shared path, we start considering the nature of emotions, and developing self-awareness by observing our assumptions, and examining how we relate to specific emotions.

It's essential for students to know that all emotions are normal, impermanent, and, in their own way, intelligent.

Students will need culturally aligned, developmentally appropriate anchor texts to interact with, along with opportunities to discuss and integrate these three key ideas.

In addition to using anchor texts and direct instruction, teachers can meet everything students express with receptivity and curiosity to help them gain confidence that their emotions are normal and acceptable. We can avoid undercutting the power of this insight by refraining from lecturing or trying to "cheer up" students before they can express the depth of their sentiments.

It's also important to emphasize that emotions are temporary. An emotion can be seen as a chemical body process that only lasts about ninety seconds. According to many psychologists, that's how long it takes for the body to react and recover.[2] Adolescents are regularly swept by powerful emotions, with hormonal spikes at times overpowering the regulating prefrontal cortex. We can encourage students to stay with the body sensations for just ninety seconds and let the energy of the emotion roll through without reacting right away.

We can also let them know they can fully feel an emotion without necessarily acting on it.

As strong emotion comes up for our students, we can witness, paraphrase, and even narrate what we are observing.

Using a scale of 1–10 for intensity can help students both in the moment and also support them in developing self-regulation. When a student is in the throes of a strong emotion, we can ask, "How strong are you feeling the emotion now, on a scale of 1–10?" We can also teach students to keep rating the intensity of an emotion as it moves through its peak of intensity.

When students reflect on how they have reacted in the throes of different feelings, it's important to encourage self-compassion coupled with self-awareness.

Many of us have been taught to repress our emotions. As a result, this territory can feel volatile at first. Especially during periods of emotional intensity in our classrooms, it is absolutely critical that we have strong personal practices to help us process what comes up and to hold it all with as much spaciousness as possible.

It may challenge us, the teachers, to work with our own difficult emotions in order to be present for the difficult emotions of our students.

It might be tempting to stay closer to the surface, and sometimes it's even skillful to do so. We need to be adept at determining when to back away from intensity, but it's also important to remember that emotional intensity can be a good sign that students are starting to move stuck emotions and heal themselves.

Some kids have many healing modalities and guides, but for others, this might be a precious chance to heal themselves and each other, clear away inner obstacles, individuate, and step into their power. It's an honor and a privilege to support kids in finding their way; and we shouldn't take this possibility lightly.

It can also be helpful to remember that people at this age are experimenting with different identities and how emotions are expressed might be part of a passing experiment. That is all fine, acceptable, and developmentally normal, too.

Once we have established the idea that all emotions are normal and temporary, we can start to teach that all emotions are actually *useful,* even and especially the difficult ones. Consciously understanding that difficult emotions have a purpose empowers us to work with them more skillfully. Fear keeps us safe. Anger alerts us when our boundaries are overstepped or when injustice needs to be addressed. Sadness connects us to the people around us.

Once students have begun to stabilize the mind by placing their attention on one thing for incrementally longer periods, and have invited the possibility of settling the nervous system, they can gradually start to cultivate the ability to remain present with their inner experiences as they arise in real time, including when difficult emotions appear.

For some students, this will be very difficult. Just starting to settle the nervous system through deep breathing will be a victory; and they will need extensive modeling and support to stay present with painful memories, guilt, regret, sadness, fear, or anger. At this point, they might even need the guidance of a mental health professional to support them in opening the doors to their internal world.

For some, there will be a period of intensity or resistance, followed by what looks and feels like a breakthrough.

For some, allowing the free flow of emotions will be a relief and a joy right from the beginning.

Although intense trauma that has not yet been processed can make mindfulness challenging at first, every one of us has the capacity to be mindful, and to cope with whatever is ours to cope with. Students need to know that we have complete confidence in their ability to stay with their experiences once they are ready; and that we will be there to support them throughout the process.

Trauma specialist Resmaa Menakem makes a distinction between "dirty pain" and "clean pain." He argues that, "Healing trauma involves recognizing, accepting, and moving through pain—clean pain." Dirty pain, in contrast, is reacting reflexively as a form of flight, fight, or freeze, and can be a response to internalized oppression.[3] Encouraging and supporting students in working with their clean pain can support them in their process of self-healing.

When students are encouraged to stay with whatever arises, paying unbiased attention even to painful and difficult emotions, they gradually enhance self-awareness as they begin to notice their personal patterns for avoiding pain and escaping discomfort, and give themselves permission to fully feel all emotions.

> **Three Things to Teach About Emotions:**
>
> 1. All emotions are **normal and acceptable**
> 2. Emotions are **temporary**
> 3. Emotions have a **purpose**

In the words of one high school student, "You'll begin to notice new things with a different mindset, a growth mindset, and have a better grip of controlling your feelings which makes you feel confident and empowered."

This perspective improves confidence, self-compassion, and resilience. In this way, mindfulness is presented as a courageous path of warriorship—and students can gradually come to see themselves as warriors of the heart.

NOTES

1. Desiree W. Murray and Katie Rosanbalm, *Promoting Self-Regulation in Adolescents and Young Adults: A Practice Brief. OPRE Report 2015-82*, Office of Planning, Research and Evaluation, January 31, 2017, https://eric.ed.gov/?id=ED594226

2. Bryan E. Robinson, "The 90-Second Rule That Builds Self-Control," *Psychology Today*, accessed August 10, 2023, https://www.psychologytoday.com/us/blog/the-right-mindset/202004/the-90-second-rule-builds-self-control

3. Resmaa Menakem, "Healing Trauma through the Body," *Omega*, April 1, 2017, https://www.eomega.org/article/healing-trauma-through-the-body

Chapter Eleven

Right Emphasis and the Importance of Emphasizing Authenticity Over Positivity

> We are only human, we all have flaws, and that's OK. Knowing this can improve our self-confidence so we are more open and honest with ourselves and the world.
>
> —Anonymous, high school student

> I'd rather be whole than good.
>
> —Carl Jung

"Your attitude determines your altitude."

"Whatever the mind can conceive and believe, it can achieve."

"The key is to see the glass as half full."

We've all heard these expressions on the power of positivity. Most of us believe that a positive mindset is important for living a good life. And most of us very much want to embody positivity, and to encourage the people around us to do the same.

But serious problems can arise when we prioritize positivity or optimism over authenticity in mindfulness instruction, especially when it comes to students who have experienced multiple traumas and might regularly experience painful emotions or have numbed out emotions entirely.

Over six years and with the support of my administrators, I created a mindfulness program at my public high school in Brooklyn, New York. We added on a little more each year in direct response to students' needs. In its fullest expression, I taught all incoming ninth grade students and supported mindfulness, Restorative Justice, and social and emotional learning practices schoolwide.

In a unit on dealing with difficult emotions, I include two lessons on toxic positivity—the idea that when we go too far with positivity, it can have dire consequences. Genuine optimism is wonderful, but toxic positivity is when we take positivity to the point that it is damaging and shuts down the rest of our emotions. One high school student wrote, "Toxic positivity is the concept that focuses on so-called positive emotions and rejects anything that may trigger negative emotions."[1]

In a 2023 study, researchers found that people who tend to judge feelings like sadness, fear, and anger as bad or wrong have more anxiety and depression symptoms than people who generally perceive their negative emotions as positive or neutral.[2] And in a 2018 survey of 70,000 people, one third of respondents said they judge themselves for having so-called "bad emotions" or actively try to push aside "bad" feelings like grief, fear, or anger.[3] This refusal to accept feelings we would prefer not to have can carry over to our children and students.

Although when we encourage students to be positive our intention might be to help, we need to be aware that we may inadvertently be causing harm. The consequences of toxic positivity include shutting down our emotions, disabling our ability to relate to others' real emotions, inhibiting our ability to form close relationships, and stopping us from seeking help when we need it. Toxic positivity can also contribute to anxiety, depression, and even suicide because when students bottle up or try to cover their real feelings, there is no way to resolve them, heal, or seek help.

If we overemphasize positivity instead of teaching our children to be authentic and empowered, we run the risk of giving them the unspoken message that something is wrong with them when difficult feelings arise—that if they just had more strength of character, they could wrestle anger, sadness, fear, self-hatred, jealousy, and anxiety to the ground with the sheer force of willpower.

Another high school student, Jamya White, wrote, "I notice that many people try to hide their real emotions with the emotions that they are told they must have."[4]

Instead of accidentally teaching students to disown their real feelings (and therefore their real selves), the antidote to toxic positivity is to emphasize authenticity instead. We can invite students to meet all emotions with an attitude of acceptance and curiosity, knowing at once that emotions are temporary and don't necessarily need to be acted out to be felt fully.

This means that we as teachers have to model acceptance and authenticity. Sometimes our rush to encourage students to look on the bright side comes up because we don't have the tools or bandwidth to deal with the emotions that come up for *us* when a student expresses strong emotions. It can seem like good intentions, but sometimes the root cause is to put a stop to the discomfort we ourselves are feeling.

My son Simon, at age nine, went through a period of negativity following eight grueling months of pandemic restrictions. Suddenly my creative, inquisitive child seemed angry, resentful, and disaffected by the things he had previously been passionate about.

I panicked. I feared for his future. As a teacher, I knew too well what can happen to kids who frequently express negativity in the classroom. I also feared that children of color, like my own precious son, were especially vulnerable to teachers with unexamined implicit biases who aren't willing to extend the benefit of doubt and I prayed his cheerful, sweet attitude would return.

My self-worth and skill as a parent also took a hit. I started lecturing him—trying to help him see how important it was for him to have a pleasant and positive attitude.

Following a period of slammed doors, guilt trips, and hurt feelings, I remembered the core teachings I'm such a big proponent of. Thankfully, I was able to shift my perspective and let Simon know that I love and accept him no matter what, even when he is experiencing difficult feelings. His whole body seemed to relax with relief. He shared that more than anything, he wanted to be positive, and that he was suffering a lot because he couldn't seem to shake the difficult thoughts and feelings.

As he settled down and gave himself permission to feel whatever he was feeling, the negativity loosened its grip and became less of a constant force.

In the words of high school student Naomi Williams, "Toxic positivity is when you feel guilty or like a burden for feeling anything other than happy. It stops you from understanding and feeling your emotions—causing you to carry around all these negative emotions, weighing down your spirit, causing you to feel self-hatred, and dragging out your period of sadness."[5]

What we choose to emphasize matters. Students, especially those who have experienced trauma, do not need another reason to feel like something is wrong with them. When we create the conditions for students to work with the full range of their real emotions, we assist them in stepping into their own self-healing and empowerment—the real work of mindfulness for youth.

Emphasizing authenticity and acceptance over positivity may be especially critical for students of color who have the added challenge of dealing with racism on a daily basis, and who may have been given the message far too many times that their feelings are not real or don't matter.

If there is a secret sauce in my classroom, this is it. Everything that you feel is totally normal and understandable. What you feel matters. What you believe matters. *You* matter. In this emotionally safer container, before long the students are the ones creating the space for one another to be real, present, and courageous.

There are many valid healing modalities available to our children, but the teaching of total acceptance for the full range of emotions is one thing that distinguishes mindfulness and makes it uniquely powerful. Undercutting it with "just look on the bright side" messages diminishes the transformative power of mindfulness.

When we accept our beautiful children in all that they are, we teach them to say yes to life, to care about their feelings and opinions, and, ironically, we might even wind up with *truly* positive children, who deeply understand their own worth and who shine from within, of their own self-blessing.[6]

NOTES

1. High school student, comment in written classwork, 2019.
2. Emily C. Willroth et al., "Judging Emotions as Good or Bad: Individual Differences and Associations with Psychological Health," *Emotion* 23, no. 7 (March 2023), https://doi.org/10.1037/emo0001220
3. Staff, "The Tyranny of Relentless Positivity," *Mindful*, February 2, 2018, https://www.mindful.org/real-gift-negative-emotions/
4. Jamya White, student comment in written classwork, 2021.
5. Naomi Williams, student comment in written classwork, 2020.
6. Galway Kinnell, "Saint Francis and the Sow," Poetry Foundation, accessed August 6, 2023, https://www.poetryfoundation.org/poems/42683/saint-francis-and-the-sow

Chapter Twelve

Culturally Responsive and Antiracist Practice

Freedom is never given; it is won.

—A. Philip Randolph

"You have to understand. You know what's hot. You know what's about to pop. You're the ones making trends. And that's really valuable. Don't let anyone tell you it isn't."

My friend, an ultra-successful marketing professional and proud Black man, stood in front of a classroom full of eleventh grade students on Career Day at my Brooklyn school.

Career Days, when outside professionals visit schools to help expose kids to different career paths, though valuable, can be chaotic and repetitive, but students were rapt with attention following this remark.

Noting the shift in energy gave me pause. It seemed likely this was a *different* message than what many had internalized, at least within school. All too often, schools communicate that students, especially students of color, are working from a deficit rather than from a place of strength and cultural richness.

That year at graduation, the valedictorian spoke with pride about all of the student entrepreneurs who had started their own businesses before even graduating from high school. I wasn't working with graduating students that year, but I had no idea about the many student entrepreneurs.

I wondered why I wasn't aware. How did I miss something so significant? Was it in part that I was deficit-oriented, rather than sustaining a lens that sees strengths and successes? Was it in part that the school, the system, the society was deficit-oriented? Was it that the students themselves didn't think to bring their successes to teachers' and school leaders' attention because they didn't think they would be valued?

For decades, scholars have shown that schools often fail to see the inherent strengths that students of color and their families bring, and fail to acknowledge the potential for academic success.

Asset-based pedagogies, such as culturally responsive teaching, focus on strengths rather than deficits. Culturally responsive teaching means setting the conditions for students to use their own values, experiences, and perspectives as an integral part of the learning process.[1]

A mindfulness classroom that is culturally responsive is nonjudgmental and nonpunitive, supports students in rich expression of their multiple identities, and respects the agency and wisdom of every student. Students are encouraged to express concepts through the lens of their own identities, and to analyze new ideas for how they measure up to their own values and priorities.

Zaretta Hammond, in *Culturally Responsive Teaching and the Brain*, argues that a culturally responsive stance also means that we work to keep students in the zone of proximal development, the optimal space of learning where every student is appropriately challenged. The author advocates a "warm demander" stance, whereby teachers demonstrate care and love for students, and at the same time show up with compelling rigor and high expectations.[2]

In addition to being culturally responsive, mindfulness classrooms must also be antiracist. To be antiracist means we are not only *not* racist but that we take an active and ongoing stance to work against narratives, structures, policies, beliefs, representations, and any other factors that contribute to racism.[3]

Obstacles to individual and group achievement are considered within the context of systemic and institutional factors; and we actively work to counter narratives that render any of our children as inherently deficient.

An antiracist classroom also shares power and wields authority without aggression and avoids misusing mindfulness instruction as a way to accomplish student compliance.

Instruction, grading, and assessment are well-structured, transparent, and clear, and encourage students' agency and engagement in the learning process, rather than relying on punitive or compliance-based practices.

Approaching all topics as food for inquiry rather than as moral imperatives, with the suggestion to investigate and see what it means for each of us individually, supports a culturally responsive and antiracist classroom.

We hold space for students to express their real experiences as well as to dream, hope, and plan for the future. The need to see the truth and understand the impact of systemic inequality is woven into our classroom practices, but we don't force it into every conversation. Instead, we support our students in showing us when they need to be real, and when they need to focus on other concerns.

I acknowledge that I have a lot to learn about culturally responsive teaching and antiracist practices. The work that I do as a mindfulness teacher is motivated primarily by the wish to empower students of color, but I am scarcely qualified to speak on this topic. I humbly offer these few suggestions because I could not write a book like this without this chapter and because I hope it can contribute, in some way, to improved practices that support every one of our students in thriving and standing in their power.

NOTES

1. Madeline Will and Ileana Najarro, "What Is Culturally Responsive Teaching?," *Education Week*, April 18, 2022, https://www.edweek.org/teaching-learning/culturally-responsive-teaching-culturally-responsive-pedagogy/2022/04

2. Zaretta Hammond, *Culturally Responsive Teaching and the Brain* (United States: Corwin/Sage, 2015).

3. Ibram X. Kendi, *How to Be an Antiracist* (New York: One World, 2019).

Chapter Thirteen

Creating Meaning with Ritual

> Our youth long for experiences that touch their innermost beings, that catapult them out of the ennui of modern culture and feed their awakening fertility, creativity, and desire to make a positive change in the world.
>
> —Melissa Michaels, PhD, *Youth on Fire:
> Birthing a Generation of Embodied Global Leaders*

Many teachers feel bombarded with new mandates, initiatives, rollouts, and requirements. It's easy to get jaded and believe that nothing is much different than anything else and that if we really get behind something, it will just get tossed out with a new superintendent anyway.

Perhaps as a result, our classroom exchanges can become primarily transactional.

This is how you write a topic sentence; this is how you solve for x; this is the role of mitochondria in a cell; illustrate and describe the steps of the research process.

But if we are willing to risk believing, and if we want our students to actually embody mindfulness, self-healing, and empowerment, we need to go beyond the merely *transactional* and cue students into the possibility of deeper meaning and personal transformation.

Excellent instruction requires the creation of systems and protocols to support learning and emotionally safer spaces but doesn't stop there. Highly effective mindfulness instruction also includes the creation of traditions, rituals, and imagery that support students in making personal meaning out of the course material and in integrating the concepts into their own schema.

A powerful section of our toolshed for making meaning and encouraging transformation is ritual.

Humans worldwide have created rituals for millennia, but in many contemporary communities ritual is not emphasized. In our secular schools we may avoid ritual entirely, fearing that it veers too close to religion. But our youth are struggling to individuate and come of age, and ritual might be exactly what they need to seek meaning and enact it in their lives in a healthy way.

In a mindfulness classroom, we can deploy the power of ritual in a variety of ways.

Our classroom routines and protocols themselves can become a kind of ritual. For example, starting and ending the class the same way every day and building respect around these routines can support students' development.

I often like to start class with a few minutes of less-structured time leading up to an opening ritual. Students might be getting settled, interacting with a prompt to engage them in the direction of the lesson, and checking in with their classmates. Then our opening ritual might be a brief meditation. If we're learning a new mindfulness technique, or if I want to expand on something we've been working with, the meditation might be teacher-led.

Most of the time, though, the opening meditation is student led. We turn the lights down, close the door, pause movement around the space, and start with a bell or a chime. It takes a long time for this to look like anything but a train wreck, but by the end of the semester, this is often the thing that students remember the most—the feeling of being in a collective field of mindfulness—and all that it opened up for them.

It is inevitably a tricky balance. If we insist too strongly, it's likely to backfire. While we work hard to cultivate a sense of reverence during key moments, it's always important to avoid being sanctimonious and to maintain a sense of humor.

In my weekly or biweekly Restorative Justice–style circle discussions, ritual is also very important. First, the action of being in circle is connected to Indigenous practices worldwide. Chairs are placed in a circle, we create a centerpiece with objects that are in some way meaningful, and we use a Talking Piece to take turns speaking. The agenda is also ritualized, and each circle starts with an opening ceremony and ends with a closing ceremony.

During the first circle, we also create class agreements that will guide us throughout the course. Class agreements are not rules but more like guiding principles that we put in place so everyone can feel safe, seen, supported, and valued to the extent possible. We revisit our agreements and occasionally revise them at the beginning of every circle, and it becomes its own kind of community ritual.

Students can also participate in the creation of meaningful openings and closings, both in circle and in daily classes.

Another element I use to help engage ritual is music. Some classes like calming music during the opening meditation. We can also put on music at the beginning of class or during independent work time. We can choose to repeat certain songs at key moments, such as at the beginning of a circle discussion, Monday morning, or when we are celebrating student achievements for the week. Being the class DJ is a role many students enjoy, and can also help to bring a sense of ceremony and meaning into the classroom.

Over the years, I've held space for a forgiveness ritual, called "Forgiveness Day," a process I learned from a colleague that has been adapted for my own students. Forgiveness Day happens only after a strong community has been established, and only after we have completed a unit on how to deal with difficult emotions and also a unit on empathy which give students tools for dealing with both their own strong emotions as well as the strong emotions of others. Leading up to Forgiveness Day, we study the science of forgiveness and engage with some personal narratives around the theme of forgiveness.

For this special ritual, we create a centerpiece that looks like a fire. Each student is given a paper with multiple prompts around "something I want to forgive someone for" or "something I want to be forgiven for" and invited to silently write their responses. There is also a prompt option that says, "Someday I hope to be able to forgive _____ for _____, even though I'm not ready yet."

We start with an opening meditation and remind students about the tools they have in place for dealing with strong emotions, including steps they have learned for what to do if they are triggered (see appendix). For Forgiveness Day, we also have at least one counselor participate and support the process.

We use a Talking Piece and each student has the option to read what they wrote, then crumple it up and put it in the "fire." They can also just read it silently in their own head, and be witnessed as they put it into the fire. Of course, they can also choose to pass.

As soon as one person authentically shares their experience, more and more have the courage to speak up, and we often have to go around multiple times. Although the process could be completed in one day, I always plan two days to make sure we have time for everyone to share to the extent that they want to.

Once, when we were having this ritual, a student hesitated, considering whether or not to speak, and another, from across the circle started to chant, "Speak your truth. Speak your truth. Speak your truth," and a few others joined in. The previously withdrawn student decided to share what was alive for her. She started to cry as she recounted what had been going on at home and how much anxiety she had been experiencing. The room was quiet as she emptied her heart. Some students tapped their hearts indicating "What you said moves my heart" or made hearts with their hands indicating "I love you." As she looked around at this show of support she started to cry harder. In the coming weeks, she started working with a counselor and making friends.

In the words of student Gayana Maelle, "I felt good starting to forgive myself. I learned that forgiveness is the best thing to do for the other person, but mostly for yourself."[1]

Creating the conditions for these kinds of moments is a very important part of my job. However, if, for any reason, "Forgiveness Day" starts to go off the rails, I'm ready to pause the ritual until we can adjust the conditions to make the safest space possible.

Forgiveness Day has to be very carefully constructed and might not be for everyone, but every teacher can contemplate how to engage and deploy ritual to support students in accessing their depths, believing in the possibility of transformation, and stepping into their own process of self-healing.

NOTE

1. Gayana Maelle, student comment in written classwork, 2022.

Chapter Fourteen

Engaging Families as Partners

> In every conceivable manner, the family is link to our past, bridge to our future.
>
> —Alex Haley, author of *Roots: The Saga of an American Family*

Working skillfully with families is the secret ingredient for teaching excellence.

A lot of what I've learned about working with families, I've learned from my mother, Betsy LeBorious, who has been immersed in the field of family engagement for decades.

In New York City, we have forty-five minutes of contractually dedicated time for "parent engagement" each week. Some teachers use this time to call to report incidents of noncompliance to parents, with the hope that parents will come down on their kids.

Over these many years, my mother has always asserted that family engagement is about establishing relationships; and if the primary communication that school representatives undertake with families is with the intention of squashing bad behavior, we are missing the mark, sending the message that we, the faces of education, know better than families, that they are doing a bad job as parents, and that they are somehow inept or incompetent.

Everyone wants to feel seen—not judged by preconceptions or scolded. When schools give the message that they are judging families, not only do the families feel judged but the students do, too. And seen through a lens of racial justice, there are even deeper ripples.

In some cases, school-based professionals tend to view families, especially families of students of color who live in low income communities, as liabilities rather than as partners.

Conversely, when teachers form strong relationships with families, not only do family members feel seen but students do, too.

There is another way. Or, rather, there are intersecting, overlapping systems that work together to offer better ways.

• • •

Elijah changed schools and joined my ninth grade mindfulness class in October during pandemic remote learning. I'd taught his sister two years previous, and I asked how she was. He was not super forthcoming. I spent a few minutes with him after the first class he joined, explaining the red tape of the class and how grading works.

I had sent all parents specific information on the class outcomes and on our first topic, as well as updates for each new topic. I reached out to his mom a few days after he joined the class to say hello, explain the purpose of the class, and share the types of things we would be working on. She also seemed somewhat guarded. I remembered meeting her briefly at an afterschool recital when I had her daughter, Elijah's older sister, and she was also guarded at that time. Whenever Elijah didn't attend class, I sent a polite text message letting his mother know I had missed him in class, and offering instructions on what he needed to complete.

Elijah's mother asked me to also include his father in any communication about Elijah. After a week or two, I reached out and asked to speak directly with Elijah. He asked, "Is this class *required*?"[1] I learned that his sister had told him not to worry about the class because it wasn't required (perhaps trying to help him since he was feeling overwhelmed?). I patiently shared the definition of mindfulness and the purpose of the class: that it is more than anything to help students step up into their power, and to actively make the world we want to live in by making the community we want. He didn't seem to be buying it, but listened politely.

Elijah started to come to class more and to stay longer. I made sure to say his name at least once during the class period, and to create opportunities for every student to speak. One day, he offered to share something he'd written in response to a reflection question and opened up a discussion. So I sent a text message to both parents saying that Elijah had been a star in mindfulness class that day. The next day, I put students in groups of four to do a brief breakout group activity. I selected a student leader from each group. "Elijah, can I please ask you to be the leader for your group?"

"Umm. Wait, what do I have to do? Umm. OK."

"I'll explain again, don't worry," I said, and then gave them a crash course in facilitation and sent them off. The students were on their own for four minutes, and I gathered that it went well in his group.

So again, I texted both parents, this time saying, "Elijah stepped up as a leader in mindfulness class today." His father wrote, "That's great news and we are so excited to hear as well as proud of him." And his mother wrote, "Thank you so much. He is really enjoying the class."

What a shift from "Is this class *required?*"

When Elijah did disengage a little, I sent a message to his parents. "I'm concerned about Elijah. He hasn't turned in work since November 23, and he hasn't been as likely to speak up lately. How can I support him?" Because we already had a strong relationship, accountability didn't seem like an accusation, and I knew I could count on his parents to collaborate with me in keeping him engaged.

The next class, Elijah was the first one to complete the classwork and turn in the assignment, and I immediately texted his parents to share his success.

• • •

First and foremost, our curriculum, instruction, grading, assessment, and feedback systems must be functioning well. We need to have clear standards and outcomes, and to have transparent, accessible systems for communicating student progress on our outcomes. A 2021 national research survey by Learning Heroes, a Carnegie Corporation grantee, found that what parents most need from their students' teachers is to understand what learning targets their student needs to meet, and how they are doing on accomplishing those targets.[2]

A clear map for what we're actually *doing* with their children is our first bridge to families. I start the year with a letter to families that defines what mindfulness is and lays out the topics we'll cover, and I also include the course standards. In the letter, I provide my contact information, encourage families to share their ideas and to collaborate, and express that I'm looking forward to getting to know their children.

As the year moves along, I reach out frequently to provide information on new units, and to offer questions they can ask their students if they want to enter into dialogue with them.

I work hard to get at least one functioning family phone number per student, and I put all of these numbers into my phone. During the first week of class, I call every single family. I introduce myself and ask if they have a few minutes to talk about the class. Next, I ask what they would like me to call them, and note it for future contact. Often, I find out that the parent has a mindfulness practice already, and has something to offer that I can share with students. In some cases, parents aren't sure what mindfulness is, so I offer a working definition and some of my favorite topics. I also ask them if there is anything it would be helpful for me to know about their child, and make careful notes. It works best to have these initial conversations right away, long before any challenges come up that we might need to address.

When a student exhibits a behavior I want to encourage, I go all out to praise them and let families know. As a teacher, I am constantly on the lookout for something to praise. I typically reach out with praise for three students following every class meeting. Doing a great job on classwork, helping out a classmate, stepping up as a leader to facilitate a breakout group, sharing a poignant piece of writing, completing an entire assignment for the first time, helping out with attendance, or anything else could lead to a positive message to parents.

These calls make me love my job. In the first round of calls, some parents hold their breath and grit their teeth, since they are used to getting bad news from schools and expect that my call is more of the same. When I'm just calling to say I'm excited to work with their student, and that they seem like a nice kid so far, they relax. After a while, parents have me in their phones, too, and we get used to regularly touching base.

• • •

I call a student's mother to share something her son wrote in an assignment. She takes my call right away and I share delightedly. He wrote, "Mindful Listening could help me build stronger relationships because if you are able to give someone your full attention by listening in a mindful way, you will be able to get to know them on a level that you otherwise would miss. The more you are able to understand someone, and vice versa, the deeper your relationship will be." She is delighted, too, and reinforces his success at home.

This particular student hadn't done written classwork for the first two marking periods, though he attended zoom classes every time. Slowly, with reinforcement, he started to complete tasks, until he finally completed an entire assignment for the first time.

Working closely with parents is the absolute best possible support for engaging reluctant students who, in many cases, have accumulated an unexamined identity as "bad" students and have learned to disengage as a way to protect themselves.

Another thing to consider is that when we engage with families, not only will we have more impact on the student, we might have opportunities to offer new skill sets and perspectives to entire families.

I once had a moving experience with a mother and daughter on the phone. The daughter, Lellia, was fairly quiet in our class meetings, and I didn't feel like I knew her very well, though our class had already been meeting for months. We had just started a unit on dealing with difficult emotions.

Lellia read the poem "The Guest House" by thirteenth-century Islamic poet Rumi; and in answer to "What advice does the poet give about dealing with difficult emotions?" she wrote, "The poet says to not let them in."[3] She had also responded to a question asking "What do you do when a difficult emotion comes up when you're practicing meditation?" with "I usually try to ignore it or push it away." This particular poem is about accepting all of our emotions—the direct opposite of her response.

I had an idea about what might be going on, and I knew I had to find a way to open the discussion around this, but really wasn't sure where to begin. So I called Lellia's mother. I began by saying I wanted to check in since we hadn't spoken for a while. I also asked if Lellia tended to be shy, as she wasn't very expressive in my class, and asked if she thought there was anything I could do to help her feel more inspired to share her ideas. The mother suggested we add Lellia to the call.

She clearly had a close and loving relationship with her daughter, and she drew her out in our conversation. At one point, she asked, "What have you been studying in class lately?" Lellia asked if I would please speak to this, and I shared some of the content from our Dealing with Difficult Emotions unit. I talked a lot about what we'd been discussing the last two days: toxic positivity. Toxic positivity is the idea that when we go too far with positivity, it can have the accidental effect of shutting down the other emotions and make it seem like not all emotions are OK.

Lellia stayed fairly quiet during this part. At the end, the mother said, "Wow, I feel like I just learned something during this phone call." We all paused. "What did you learn?" I asked. "I'm always very big on positivity. I always say we have to be positive, no matter what. But it never occurred to me that it might mean that we don't express the other emotions. I think this is something we could work on as a family, learning to express all of our emotions more."

Let me be clear, this was a set of conditions that I had very little input in. No doubt Lellia's mother and Lellia herself had already been involved in their own processes of healing. But the strong relationship I had already established with Lellia's mother allowed me to enter into this sensitive conversation. This time, curriculum and instruction created the framework to see what might be happening, intuition guided me to address it, and skillfulness helped me to address it delicately, relying on the respectful, collaborative relationship we had worked to build.

This is what's possible when we engage not only students but their families as partners, when we realize that we are not the authority but simply the agent who is holding space, and doing what we can to create the conditions for transformation and healing.

NOTES

1. Elijah, student verbal comment, 2020. Name changed for anonymity.
2. Eyal Bergman, *Unlocking the How: Designing Family Engagement Strategies That Lead to Success*, Learning Heroes, March 2022, https://bealearninghero.org/wp-content/uploads/2023/07/Learning-Heroes_Parents-report22_Appendix_v7.pdf
3. Ibid.

Conclusion

May this book support your practice.
May you have many opportunities to witness and experience beauty.
May you have many blessings on your path.
May you and your students thrive;
And may every child stand in their power and reach their full potential.

Appendix A: Meditation Techniques and Basic Instructions

BREATH-CENTERED MEDITATION:

- Take a mindful posture, a body position that feels both powerful and relaxed.
- Bring attention to the physical sensations of the body, for example the weight of the body in your chair or cushion, the feeling of the feet on the floor, or the feeling of clothes touching the skin.
- Take a deep breath in, and let your attention rest on the sound of the bell as you breathe out.
- Notice the place you feel the breath the most strongly, and bring your attention to that place, perhaps even bringing your hand there.
- Take a few deep, slow breaths, then see if you can let the attention be on the feeling of the body breathing, as it moves the anchor place.
- When your attention goes to something else, notice that, then when you are ready, gently bring the attention back to the feeling of the body breathing. Don't be too harsh with this part; it's totally normal for different thoughts and feelings to come.

BREATH-CENTERED MEDIATION VARIATION—
THREE-PART BREATHING:

- Pre-practice: Invite students to breathe just into the belly, and debrief. Then breathe just into the ribcage, and debrief. Next, breathe just into the chest, and debrief. Encourage students to exaggerate at this stage.
- Take a mindful posture, a body position that feels both powerful and relaxed.

- Bring attention to the physical sensations of the body, for example the weight of the body in your chair or cushion, the feeling of the feet on the floor, or the feeling of clothes touching the skin.
- Take a deep breath in, and let your attention rest on the sound of the bell as you breathe out.
- Take a few deep, slow breaths, then see if you can let the attention be on the feeling of the body breathing, as it moves the anchor place.
- When your attention goes to something else, notice that, then when you are ready, gently bring the attention back to the feeling of the body breathing. Don't be too harsh with this part; it's totally normal for different thoughts and feelings to come.
- See if you can move the breath in through three different places, first into the belly, then into the ribcage, then into the chest. Then, release the breath from the chest, the ribcage, and the belly.

BREATH-CENTERED MEDIATION VARIATION— COUNTING BREATHS:

- Pre-practice: Demonstrate how to count each time you breathe slowly out.
- Take a mindful posture, a body position that feels both powerful and relaxed.
- Bring attention to the physical sensations of the body.
- Take a deep breath in, and let your attention rest on the sound of the bell as you breathe out.
- Take a few deep, slow breaths, then see if you can let the attention be on the feeling of the body breathing, as it moves the anchor place.
- Once your breath begins to feel settled, begin to count each time you breathe out. If you lose track, just notice that you lost track and start again with the number one.

SOUND-CENTERED MEDITATION:

- Take a mindful posture, a body position that feels both powerful and relaxed.
- Bring attention to the physical sensations of the body.
- Place attention on the sound of the bell and see if you can keep your mind on the sound as it fades away.
- Open your attention to all sounds that reach your ears.

- Notice when your mind is doing something different than paying attention to sound, and see if you can gently bring your attention back to sound.

LOVING-KINDNESS MEDITATION:

- Take a mindful posture, a body position that feels both powerful and relaxed.
- Bring attention to the physical sensations of the body.
- Place attention on the sound of the bell and see if you can keep your mind on the sound as it fades away.
- Bring someone you love to your mind. This could be a parent, caregiver, friend, relative, or anyone else. It could also be a pet or a famous person if no one comes to mind. Try to see this person in detail in front of you.
- Inside your head, say to this person, "May you be safe."
- Inside your head, say to this person, "May you be happy."
- Inside your head, say to this person, "May you be healthy."
- Inside your head, say to this person, "May you be peaceful."
- Keep repeating these sentences, directing them toward your mental image of this person.
- If your mind starts doing something different than repeating these sentences, see if you can gently bring your attention back to saying these sentences.

SELF-COMPASSION MEDITATION (ADAPTED FROM A PRACTICE BY DR. KRISTIN NEFF):

- Think of a situation in your life that is giving you stress or discomfort, pause to notice how your body feels and let the feeling in. Then say, "Ouch. This hurts."
- Say, "I'm not alone. We all struggle in our lives" and think about the fact that every being, even animals, experiences struggle sometimes.
- Put your hand on your heart or chest and say, "May I be kind to myself." (Or you can say what your own self most needs to hear, such as "May I accept myself" or "May I forgive myself.")

Appendix B: Mindful Minute Student Script

Mindful Minute Student Script

*****Student Instructions: You don't need to say all of these things. Just pick a few for each step. Feel free to add your own ideas. Keep in mind that it is very important to pause frequently to let people have time to experience what you say. Good luck and thank you for stepping up as a leader!

#	Step	Ideas for things I could say (choose 2–3):
Ring 1	**Mindful Body/ Mindful Posture**	It's time to return to our seats Let's pause our conversations for now Let's put down pens and pencils for now Sit up into your power Sit like the royalty you are Let your body be in a shape that is both relaxed and alert at the same time Notice how your body is feeling today Notice if any part of your body feels tense and see if it's possible to relax it Feel your feet on the floor Notice the weight of your body in the chair Notice if you're sitting straight or if your body is twisted around
Ring 2	**Sound**	Take a big breath in, and now let's turn our attention to the sound of the bell Try to keep your mind focused on the bell sound until it disappears Open your attention to all the sounds inside and outside the room Let all the sounds around you come to your ears

(continued)

#	Step	Ideas for things I could say (choose 2–3):
Ring 3	**Breath**	Now let's bring our attention to the breath
		Let's take a big breath in, expanding, filling up the lungs with air, then letting it out slowly, emptying, melting your body down
		Breathe in, noticing the upper back stretching, the belly expanding with air, the feeling of air coming in through the nose, Breathe out, noticing the belly emptying of air, the feeling of air going out the nose
		Try to keep your attention on the actual FEELING of the body breathing
		See if you can keep your attention on the entire breath from the beginning when you breath out, then the slight pause when you are empty, then the breathing in, then the slight pause when you are full of air
		See if you can notice all of the different sensations of breathing
		If you get distracted, you can just gently bring your mind back to the next breath out
*****	**Freestyle**	**Optional:**
		Add your own spin! Use your intuition and creativity to add whatever you think is needed in the moment
		(Examples of things you could make up to say:
		Remember that you are perfect and that you already have everything you need to be whole . . . put your hand on your own heart and see if you can feel your heartbeat . . . recognize that doing this work is powerful self-healing)
Ring 4	**End of Mindful Minute**	Thank you for your patience and attention. Now the Mindful Minute is done

Appendix C: Mindfulness Elective—Sample Scope and Sequence

Mindfulness Elective—Sample Scope and Sequence

Topic 1:	Notes:
Personal and Collective Identity and Community Building	In this unit, students consider their individual and collective identities and how they impact what we believe and how we behave. Students learn the grading policy, practice class protocols, learn trauma-influenced steps for dealing with difficult emotions if they arise in practice, and review the mindfulness standards. In addition, students learn fundamental brain science as it relates to mindfulness. Students also begin to develop a basic definition of mindfulness, and to engage with mindfulness of posture, mindfulness of sound, and mindfulness of breath. In addition, students will create vision boards and set personal and academic goals. (Also vocab systems, classwork systems, grading systems orientation)
Topic 2:	**Notes:**
Pausing	In this unit, students experiment with the concept of pausing as a strategy for emotional regulation through poetry, group discussion, movement, the creation of posters, and reflection. **Mindfulness Standards 3, 9, 10**
Topic 3:	**Notes:**
Flow	In this unit, students consider the topic of flow: what is a flow state, why it might be desirable, and how to cultivate flow states. Students read articles on George Mumford, the NBA mindfulness coach, and reflect on how mindfulness helps players develop flow. Students also continue to engage with breath-centered mindfulness practices with targeted lens for inquiry. (Note: include key qualities that support mindfulness lesson in this unit) **Mindfulness Standards 2, 9, 10**

(continued)

Topic 4:	Notes:
Healthy Habits	In this unit, students consider how to create routines and habits. Sleep routines, creating usable schedules, mindful eating, and exercise are considered. Later, in the Dealing with Difficult Emotions unit, students revisit Healthy Habits with a lens toward how to interrupt and defuse undesirable habits such as anxiety, self-abusive talk, and quick frustration responses. (Possibly include two lessons on the Science of Perception using the series on Disney+) **Mindfulness Standards 2, 10**

Topic 5:	Notes:
Gratitude	In this mini-unit, students consider how to cultivate habits of mind that support mindfulness practice and personal growth. Students consider the science of gratitude and how it might impact their own experience, create an artwork with things they are grateful for, and join together for a circle discussion on gratitude right before the Thanksgiving break. **Mindfulness Standard 10**

Topic 6:	Notes:
Mindful Communication	In this unit, students learn and practice mindful communication skills including paying good attention, providing encouragement, paraphrasing, reflecting/acknowledging feelings, and practicing mindfulness in conversation through videos, written reflection, and role playing. In addition, students learn and apply the perspective of Nonviolent Communication (NVC) and learn a protocol for expressing our needs directly and without causing harm. **Mindfulness Standards 11, 12**

Topic 7:	Notes:
Dealing with Difficult Emotions	In this unit, students begin to develop a range of strategies for regulating emotional states and coping with difficult emotions, such as sadness, anger, fear, and jealousy. Students learn the fight/flight/freeze construct and build on their knowledge of naming emotions ("Name it to tame it"). Students use the Center for Nonviolent Communication list of possible emotions and the classroom word wall and play a round of "feeling charades" using this list, and deepen their knowledge of mindfulness and brain science. Students also learn the "counting breaths" technique for emotional regulation and apply pausing, mindfulness of body, basic mindful communication skills, and the technique of Mindful Walking/Walking Meditation. Students are encouraged to accept all emotions and to find ways to express the full range of emotions. Students also revisit the routines they created in topic 4, and consider the idea of how we create or dismantle habitual patterns, including both daily habits and emotions that plague us. Students also collectively watch the movie *Inside Out*. Through written questions, class discussion, and reflection, students consider emotional regulation strategies and big questions about what makes us who we are. **Mindfulness Standards 3, 9, 10**

Appendix C: Mindfulness Elective—Sample Scope and Sequence

Topic 8:	Notes:
Growth Mindset	During this week, students consider the concept of growth mindset. They play a team building game with marshmallows and spaghetti, and connect the game to the concept of growth mindset. Students also read an article, watch videos, compare and contrast growth and fixed mindsets, and reflect on how having a growth mindset has the potential for positive impact. **Mindfulness Standards 6, 9, 10**
Topic 9:	Notes:
Stress, Anxiety and Self-Compassion	In this unit, students delve into stress, how it impacts us, and how to mitigate its impacts on our mental and physical health. Students also learn to create and adjust routines that include self-care and reflection in daily life. In addition, students learn counterstrategies for managing stress, such as self-compassion practice. More strategies for settling the body in the style of Resmaa Menakem are discussed and there is also a lesson on grounding. **Mindfulness Standards 2, 3, 9, 10**
Topic 10:	Notes:
Empathy	In this unit, students develop the ability to take the perspective of and empathize with others, including those from diverse backgrounds and cultures. Students analyze a song with multiple viewpoints, respond to and discuss videos, and also work in small groups on a "case study" project that allows them to carefully consider the experience and needs of one individual. Students also learn the concept of "othering" and consider what other "empathy-blockers" stop people from feeling empathy, and what political implications this has. Students consider how mindful communication supports empathy. The topic of interdependence is also introduced. **Mindfulness Standards 8, 9, 10, 11**
Topic 11:	Notes:
The Science of Forgiveness	In this mini-unit, students read an article or watch a video about the science of forgiveness and engage in a community healing ritual called "Forgiveness Day." **Mindfulness Standards 2, 9, 11**
Topic 12:	Notes:
Healthy Relationships	Students investigate the qualities of healthy and unhealthy relationships through reading, role plays, reflection, and discussion with a lens of inclusiveness. Students review and relate all of the mindfulness standards to the topic of Healthy Relationships. **Mindfulness Standards 7, 9, 10**

(continued)

Appendix C: Mindfulness Elective—Sample Scope and Sequence

Topic 13:	Notes:
Responsible Decision Making	In this unit, students expand their abilities to define problems, analyze situations, brainstorm and evaluate possible solutions, and to reflect on previous choices to make constructive decisions that are based on both individual needs and community needs. **Mindfulness Standards 7, 9, 10**
Topic 14:	**Notes:**
Speak Your Truth	In this unit, students consider the social justice implications of mindfulness as empowerment for all, and what it means to step up into our power. Students also examine oppressive systems and what beliefs and structures sustain them. Students also reflect on and share what issues are most important to them and why. **Mindfulness Standards 10, 12**
Topic 15:	**Notes:**
Final Project	Students review and evaluate what they have learned throughout the year; and create new materials using selected class concepts.

Appendix D: Sample Mindfulness Course Standards

Sample Mindfulness Course Standards

1	Identity	The ability to examine personal identities and collective identities in order to understand how both impact what we believe and how we act
2	Self-Awareness	The ability to recognize our emotions, thoughts, and body sensations and how they influence behavior, including how past experiences might still influence today's behaviors, in order to respond constructively to situations as they arise
3	Emotional Self-Regulation	The ability to utilize a range of strategies for emotional self-regulation, including impulse control, pausing, and managing difficult emotions like sadness, anxiety, and anger, in order to manage mood and energy level constructively
4	Responsible Decision Making	The ability to define problems, analyze situations, brainstorm and evaluate possible solutions, and reflect on previous choices to make constructive decisions that are based on both individual needs and community needs in order to improve the outcomes of decisions
5	Visualization	The ability to set goals, clarify intentions, and visualize desired outcomes in order to achieve our potential
6	Growth Mindset	The ability to identify areas of strength and build on existing skills; and the ability to identify areas that need improvement and to approach these areas with optimism and motivation in order to grow and evolve
7	Healthy Relationships	The ability to establish and maintain healthy and rewarding relationships, including the ability to express our needs and feelings, to listen mindfully, to manage conflict constructively, and to resist inappropriate peer pressure

(continued)

8	**Empathy**	The ability to take the perspective of and empathize with others, including those from diverse backgrounds and cultures, in order to feel connected to our friends, families, and communities
9	**Language**	The ability to participate in discussions using vocabulary specific to mindfulness, including using nuanced words that specifically define emotions in order to expand our expressive range and name emerging emotions as they arise
10	**Reflection**	The ability to reflect—both verbally and in writing—on how mindfulness has the potential to positively impact emotional well-being in order to refine and expand our mindfulness strategies
11	**Communication: Listening**	The ability to identify and utilize key listening strategies, including paying good attention, providing encouragement, paraphrasing, and practicing mindfulness in order to improve our relationships
12	**Communication: Speaking**	The ability to identify and utilize key speaking strategies, including pausing, choosing your words, paying attention to your listener(s), and practicing mindfulness in order to improve our relationships

Appendix E: Steps for What Students Can Do If Triggered During Practice

1. *Notice* that you feel something
2. *Pause* and list everything you can notice (heart beating fast, sweating, breathing, etc.)
3. *Decide* if you will still do the experiment the class is doing or if you will do something different
4. *Get support* if needed

Bibliography

Bauer, Clemens C., Camila Caballero, Ethan Scherer, Martin R. West, Michael D. Mrazek, Dawa T. Phillips, Susan Whitfield-Gabrieli, and John D. E. Gabrieli. "Mindfulness Training Reduces Stress and Amygdala Reactivity to Fearful Faces in Middle-school Children." *American Psychological Association* 133, no. 6 (December 2019): 569–85. https://doi.org/10.1037/bne0000337.

Bergman, Eyal. *Unlocking the How: Designing Family Engagement Strategies That Lead to Success.* Learning Heroes, March 2022. https://bealearninghero.org/wp-content/uploads/2023/07/Learning-Heroes_Parents-report22_Appendix_v7.pdf

Brensliver, Matthew, JoAnna Hardy, and Oren Jay Sofer. *Teaching Mindfulness to Empower Adolescents.* New York: W. W. Norton, 2020.

CASEL. "What Is the CASEL Framework?" Accessed March 3, 2023. https://casel.org/fundamentals-of-sel/what-is-the-casel-framework/.

Chiesa, Alberto, and Alessandro Serretti. "Mindfulness-Based Stress Reduction for Stress Management in Healthy People: A Review and Meta-Analysis." *Journal of Alternative and Complementary Medicine* 15, no. 5 (May 2009): 593–600. https://doi.org/10.1089/acm.2008.0495.

Davis, Fania E. *The Little Book of Race and Restorative Justice.* New York: Good Books, 2019.

DiAngelo, Robin. *White Fragility.* New York: Public Science, 2016.

Dweck, Carol. *Mindset: The New Psychology of Success.* New York: Ballantine Books, 2016.

Gunaratana, Bhante. *Mindfulness in Plain English.* Somerville: Wisdom, 2019.

Hammond, Zaretta. *Culturally Responsive Teaching and the Brain.* United States: Corwin/Sage, 2015.

Hanh, Thich Nhat. *True Love: A Practice for Awakening the Heart.* Boulder: Shambhala, 2006.

Hertz, Marci, Melissa Heim Viox, Greta M. Massetti, Kayla N. Anderson, Sarah Bacon, Erin Fordyce, Melissa C. Mercado, and Jorge V. Verlenden. "Adverse Childhood Experiences among US Adolescents Over the Course of the COVID-19

Pandemic." *Pediatrics* 151, no. 6 (June 2023): 1–9. https://doi.org/10.1542/peds.2022-060799.

Hölzel, Britta K., James Carmody, Mark Vangel, Christina Congleton, Sita M. Yerramsetti, Tim Gard, and Sara W. Lazar. "Mindfulness Practice Leads to Increases in Regional Brain Gray Matter Density." *Psychiatry Research: Neuroimaging* 191, no. 1 (January 2011): 36–43. https://doi.org/10.1016/j.pscychresns.2010.08.006.

Ivey-Stephenson, Asha V., Zewditu Demissie, Alexander E. Crosby, Deborah M. Stone, Elizabeth Gaylor, Natalie Wilkins, Richard Lowry, and Margaret Brown. "Suicidal Ideation and Behaviors among High School Students—Youth Risk Behavior Survey, United States, 2019." *MMWR Supplements* 69, no. 1 (August 21, 2020): 47–55. Centers for Disease Control and Prevention. https://www.cdc.gov/mmwr/volumes/69/su/su6901a6.htm

Jones, Sherry Everett. Kathleen A. Ethier, Marci Hertz, Sarah DeGue, Vi Donna Le, Jemekia Thornton, Connie Lim, Patricia J. Dittus, and Sindhura Geda. "Mental Health, Suicidality, and Connectedness Among High School Students During the COVID-19 Pandemic—Adolescent Behaviors and Experiences Survey, United States, January–June 2021." *MMWR Supplements* 71, no. 3 (April 1, 2022): 16–21. Centers for Disease Control and Prevention. https://www.cdc.gov/mmwr/volumes/71/su/su7103a3.htm#:~:text=and%20Mental%20Health-,Compared%20with%20those%20who%20did%20not%20feel%20close%20to%20persons,35.4%25%20versus%2052.9%25)%2C%20of

Kendi, Ibram X. *How to Be an Antiracist.* New York: One World, 2019.

Keysers, Christian, and Valeria Gazzola. "Hebbian Learning and Predictive Mirror Neurons for Actions, Sensations and Emotions," *Philosophical Transactions of the Royal B* 369, no. 1644 (June 2014): 1–11. https://doi.org/10.1098/rstb.2013.0175.

Kinnell, Galway. "Saint Francis and the Sow." Poetry Foundation, accessed August 6, 2023. https://www.poetryfoundation.org/poems/42683/saint-francis-and-the-sow

Living Justice Press. "Free Stuff." February 13, 2023. https://livingjusticepress.org/free-stuff/

McDonald, David, Danielle Ross, Andre Ross, and Shontoria Walker. (Kevin Parr quote). "3." Essay. In *Culture to the Max!: Culturally Responsive Teaching and Practice*. Hoboken: Jossey-Bass, 2022.

Menakem, Resmaa. "Healing Trauma through the Body." *Omega*, April 1, 2017. https://www.eomega.org/article/healing-trauma-through-the-body

———. *My Grandmother's Hands: Racialized Trauma and the Pathway to Mending Our Hearts and Bodies*. London: Penguin, 2021.

Mental Health America. "Racial Trauma." Accessed August 8, 2023. https://www.mhanational.org/racial-trauma

Michaels, Melissa PhD. *Youth on Fire: Birthing a Generation of Embodied Global Leaders*. Boulder: Golden Bridge, 2017.

Muhammad, Gholdy. *Cultivating Genius: An Equity Framework for Culturally and Historically Responsive Literacy*. United States: Scholastic, 2020.

Murray, Desiree W., and Katie Rosanbalm. *Promoting Self-Regulation in Adolescents and Young Adults: A Practice Brief. OPRE Report 2015-82*. Office of Planning, Research and Evaluation, January 31, 2017. https://eric.ed.gov/?id=ED594226

Neff, Kristin. "Compassion." Self-Compassion, May 30, 2023. https://self-compassion.org/

New York State Department of Education. "New York State Social Emotional Learning Benchmarks." Student Support Services. Social Emotional Learning. NYSED Documents. Accessed August 6, 2023. https://www.p12.nysed.gov/sss/sel.html

O'Driscoll, Kari. *Happy, Healthy Teens: Why Focusing on Relationships Works.* Lanham, MD: Rowman & Littlefield, 2022.

Robinson, Bryan E. "The 90-Second Rule That Builds Self-Control." *Psychology Today*, accessed August 10, 2023. https://www.psychologytoday.com/us/blog/the-right-mindset/202004/the-90-second-rule-builds-self-control

Roemer, Lizabeth, Sarah Krill Williston, and Laura Grace Rollins. "Mindfulness and Emotion Regulation." *Current Opinion in Psychology* 3 (June 2015): 52–57. https://doi.org/10.1016/j.copsyc.2015.02.006

Roth, Gabrielle, and John Loudon. *Maps to Ecstasy: Teachings of an Urban Shaman.* London: Thorsons, 1995.

Staff. "The Tyranny of Relentless Positivity." *Mindful*, February 2, 2018. https://www.mindful.org/real-gift-negative-emotions/

Tandon, Pax. *Mindfulness Matters: A Guide to Mastering Your Life.* Atglen, PA: Shiffler, 2018.

Trafton, Anne. "Two Studies Reveal Benefits of Mindfulness for Middle School Students." MIT News, August 26, 2019. https://news.mit.edu/2019/mindfulness-mental-health-benefits-students-0826

van der Kolk, Bessel. *The Body Keeps the Score: Mind, Brain and Body in the Transformation of Trauma.* London: Penguin, 2015.

Wilde, Stephanie, Anna Sonley, Catherine Crane, Tamsin Ford, Anam Raja, James Robson, Laura Taylor, and Willem Kuyken. "Mindfulness Training in UK Secondary Schools: A Multiple Case Study Approach to Identification of Cornerstones of Implementation." *Mindfulness* 10, no. 4 (June 4, 2019). https://www.ncbi.nlm.nih.gov/pmc/articles/PMC6558285/

Will, Madeline, and Ileana Najarro. "What Is Culturally Responsive Teaching?" *Education Week*, April 18, 2022. https://www.edweek.org/teaching-learning/culturally-responsive-teaching-culturally-responsive-pedagogy/2022/04

Willroth, Emily C., Gerald Young, Maya Tamir, and Iris B. Mauss. "Judging Emotions as Good or Bad: Individual Differences and Associations with Psychological Health." *Emotion* 23, no. 7 (March 2023). https://doi.org/10.1037/emo0001220

Winston, Diana. *Wide Awake: A Buddhist Guide for Teens.* New York: Penguin, 2003.

Zhang, Xiaoyan, and Shannon M. Monnat. "Racial/Ethnic Differences in Clusters of Adverse Childhood Experiences and Associations with Adolescent Mental Health." *SSM—Population Health* 17, no. 100997 (December 2021): 1–9. https://doi.org/10.1016/j.ssmph.2021.100997.

Zhou, Xiang, Jieyu Guo, Guangli Lu, Chaoran Chen, Zhenxing Xie, Jiangmin Liu, and Chuning Zhang. "Effects of Mindfulness-Based Stress Reduction on Anxiety Symptoms in Young People: A Systematic Review and Meta-Analysis." *Psychiatry Research* 289, no. 113002 (July 2020). https://doi.org/10.1016/j.psychres.2020.113002.

www.ingramcontent.com/pod-product-compliance
Lightning Source LLC
Chambersburg PA
CBHW032216230426
43672CB00011B/2575